WORLDS TORN ASUNDER

By

DOV BERIL EDELSTEIN

Library of Congress Cataloging in Publication Data

Edelstein, Dov Beril.
  Worlds torn asunder.

ISBN 978-0-88125-040-4

MANUFACTURED IN THE UNITED STATES OF AMERICA

Contents

Preface

This is not a Holocaust book. It does not record the horrifying atrocities, the barbarities, the mass killings. These, the author believes, have already been adequately documented by eyewitnesses and researchers.

The present volume is rather a microcosm of the great picture as seen introspectively by one youth who was torn away from his sheltered and comforting environment, and violently thrown into a cold, merciless, incomprehensible reality.

Steeped in Jewish lore and tradition, the Talmud-student-turned-captive interprets his personal vicissitudes in the light of the ancient traditions of his people and their historical experience. The horrifying present is somewhat mitigated by putting it into historical perspective, drawing profusely upon the Bible, Talmud, and Midrash.

What places this volume into a category of its own is its unique Jewishness. Even in the pit of utmost darkness and human degradation, Jewish faith and Jewish values asserted themselves, lending spiritual support and rendering life meaningful.

Worlds Torn Asunder depicts the richness of Jewish life in Hungary as experienced by the author during the last decade prior to the Holocaust. Woven into the dynamics of everyday life, all the major and minor festivals, as well as a great array of customs and traditions, are touched upon from a unique point of view.

Worlds Torn Asunder is a direct outgrowth of hundreds of encounters with thousands of high school and college students during the past twenty years.

Ostensibly we met to discuss Judaism. I told my eager listeners about Jewish history, religion, customs, and ethics. At the beginning, in the early sixties, no one ever dared ask me about the Holocaust; the subject, they thought, was anathema, too painful, too hurting to talk about.

With the passage of time, the ice gradually melted away. The natural eagerness, the psychological need to know what had happened there in that inferno came to the fore. I encouraged them to ask; they did.

They sat there stunned, dumbfounded, disturbed, and deeply pained that human beings, highly civilized human beings, were capable of perpetrating such heinous crimes against other human beings, even on children.

Yet, every encounter left me with the feeling that a cleansing catharsis had been effected upon my impressionable listeners. This feeling became even more evident when I read the hundreds of letters I received from my audiences following such encounters.

The sincere outpouring of warm sympathy and friendship in those letters more than compensated for the need to repeatedly talk of my unpleasant experiences.

Some students did not stop at that. Seizing the opportunity, they laid bare their own and their parents' prejudices, which until then they had taken for granted, seeing nothing wrong in them.

The following selections from students' letters are representative of most of the letters I received.

> I am no longer prejudiced against anyone anymore. I may not like some of the things some people are doing, but I sure don't hate them for it.

> I have never in my whole life met a Jewish person; now I am glad that I have. I told my parents about your coming to my school. All they said was, "that's nice." I wish they would have come and seen you.

> You said some things that made me think, like what you said about people trying to force their ideas and beliefs on others. I never realized that we all did that until now.

> It is good that you have no bad feelings toward German people. Sometimes it is much better to forgive even though it may be hard.

> I really do appreciate your coming to our class. It was a time and a day of my life I'll always remember. I hope you go to other schools and do the same thing.

If I still had doubts lingering in my mind as to the usefulness and the importance of talking to young Americans on the sufferings and injustices of the past, the following statement in one of the letters from a high school student entirely dissipated all such doubts. That sincere expression of regret strengthened my determination to tell and repeat the story as long as there are those who are willing to listen.

I wish I could go back in time and change all the hurt and unhappiness that have occurred.

Another student deeply moved me by his statement that he pitied the murderers for having sunk so low as to forfeit their human image. Unknowingly, this student echoed the famed Hebrew poet Bialik, himself an eyewitness to pogroms in Russia.

> I mused, with hate I have been sated long.
> I planted love but reaped abuse and woe.
> Than be with lions, with lambs I would rather perish.

Maybe the older generation can no longer be reeducated; perhaps prejudice and bigotry have seeped too deep into the marrow of their bones. Yet we are not free to desist from trying to immunize the younger generation from the venom of hatred. True, it is much easier to induce people to hate and to hurt than to make them love and respect. Yet, for the sake of our future, the future of all of us, for the sake of our children, the children of all nations and races, we are not at liberty not to embark on the arduous task of spreading friendship, compassion, respect, love. Otherwise we shall be doomed to relive the curses of the past again and again.

The author fervently hopes that this slim volume may serve as a humble contribution toward the attainment of the above-mentioned goal.

Although primarily recommended to high school and college students, this book should prove enlightening and worthwhile reading for sensitive people of all ages.

Acknowledgments

I would like to thank Professor Michael Kerestesi, College of Education, Wayne State University, and Dr. Menahem Schmelzer, Head Librarian, Jewish Theological Seminary of America, for having read the entire manuscript, and for their wholehearted encouragement.

I also wish to thank the following persons who read sections of the manuscript and shared with me their valuable remarks: Dr. Menahem Mansoor, Professor Emeritus and Chairman, Department of Hebrew and Semitic Studies, University of Wisconsin–Madison; Professor Patricia Drury, Department of History, Delta College; Professor Clair Harman, Department of English, Delta College; and Dr. Stephen Konowalow, Counselor at Delta College.

I would like to thank Jane Llewellyn Stoesser and Jane Corcoran for their helpful editing of several chapters; Mr. Robert Milch for his professional copy-editing; Shirley Beyett and Jan Waldman for their typing.

Special thanks go to the following persons whose generous financial assistance made possible the publication of this book: Emery and Roberta Grosinger, Robert and Elaine Hirschfield, Arnold and Sylvia Cohodas (in memory of Sarah Casper), Mark and Judy Jaffe, Sybil and Sherman Kahn (in memory of their parents Mary and George), Dr. Simon and Eva Cherkasky, Iva and Abe Goldin.

1

Childhood Years

YOU WOULDN'T FIND the name on a conventional map. Although only twelve kilometers from the metropolis city of Szatmár, the tiny hamlet of Berek, my birthplace, seemed to me to be situated at the world's hem. Like many of the peasants' houses, ours too was covered with a heavy layer of straw. Every year at springtime, a stork would build her nest on the most elevated spot in the center of our roof. Mother used to warn us children that to disturb or just to frighten the stork would be considered a grave sin. The stork, mother told us, deserved all of our attention and protection, since it was the stork that had carried water in its long beak and poured it on the flames of the Temple at the time of the Babylonian conflagration. Hence its name in Hebrew, *chassidah*, "the benevolent one."

Afterwards, whenever I saw this huge bird leaning on one foot with its head lowered, I was sure it was praying for the coming of the Messiah and the rebuilding of the Temple.

Not far from where the Gypsies lived, toward the northern reaches of our village, there was the Great Forest. Its huge, tall trees, the entangled brush, the sweet symphony of thousands of birds, the play of shade and sunshine, and the mysterious silence exerted on me a deep spell of enchantment. The Great Forest of Berek represented to my childish mind a world set apart, a world filled with wonder and splendor. At times I wondered whether it might be possible, by venturing toward the end of the forest, to eventually reach the awesome river Sambatyon, beyond which lie the glorious lands of the Ten Tribes and the sons of Moses.

Although very young, perhaps three or four years old, when I first heard the story from my father, its poignant impression never departed from my fertile, imaginative mind. I took great pride and joy in the knowledge that somewhere, far away, beyond the river Sambatyon and beyond the Dark Mountains there were broad vistas

1

flooded with sunshine and with marvels of nature. There, beyond the river and the mountains, were the lands of the free Jews, Jews who had never experienced the taste of exile, nor known the bitter yoke of the oppressor. Those free Jews were strong and brave, and as tall as the trees of the forest. In time of peace they tilled the soil and tended their sheep. Should they be attacked by an enemy, they immediately transformed into military formations of cavalry and infantry and went to meet the foe. Their spears, bows, and arrows possessed miraculous qualities, so that the enemy was defeated regardless of his numbers and strength. Needless to say, the tribes were ruled by kings of their own choice, and the high priest wore on his breastplate the holy oracle, the Urim and Thummim.

If I withstood the temptation of crossing the Great Forest and reaching the Sambatyon, it was only out of concern that if I could not return from there, I would cause great anguish to my parents. Besides, I was terrified of the boiling stones and flames that the river spewed out for twenty-four hours daily, except on the Sabbath.

On the eastern outskirts of our village there was a small river, a real river. It did not spew stones and flames, but teemed with many species of fish. On Thursdays I would accompany my older brothers to the river, where they tried their luck at catching fish for the Sabbath. Because they are always silent and of a contemplative mood, mystics and Chassidim consider it meritorious to serve a dish of fish for the Sabbath meal.

Mother had a reason of her own to rejoice when her sons met fortune and brought home a large catch of fish. Her budget, meager as it was, hardly sufficed for the most basic necessities. Meat and similar luxuries were served only on the Sabbath, and then only in small quantities. It was no mean task to feed seven hungry mouths plus a guest or two from among the seasonal drifters who chanced to our hamlet for the Sabbath and were invited to our home. Four or five large, contemplative fish would go a long way in quieting the hungry appetites of our large family.

On Friday afternoons in the summer, all the Jewish men would go to our little river for the purpose of immersing themselves in its cleansing waters in honor of the approaching Sabbath. We would go into the water naked in order to effect a perfect immersion, without anything interposing between the body and the water.

The non-Jewish inhabitants of Berek were well aware of this practice and kept away from that area of the river on Friday afternoons so as not to interfere with our religious customs.

Berek's inhabitants were served by three houses of worship. The majority was affiliated with the Greek Orthodox church. On a beautiful hill bordered by huge chestnut trees stood the Reformed church. With this church were affiliated the more intellectual segment of Berek's Christians. Not far from the village fountain stood the synagogue, where father was the rabbi and spiritual leader. His flock was very small, no more than two dozen families, most of which had a good number of children but not enough money to pay the rabbi's meager salary on time.

Father had established cordial relations with the minister of the Reformed church, who lived not far from our home. The fact that both ministered to members of minority religions no doubt played a role in the forging of their relationship. Yet there was another factor: the minister was a learned man, and he liked to discuss with father passages from the Bible and other points of interest in Jewish lore.

All year long, relations between the several Jewish families and the gentile majority were cordial, often even friendly. Father did not object if we, his children, occasionally attended a social function at the Reformed church, as it did not display crucifixes or icons. Non-Jews frequented our homes and we theirs.

A sudden and dramatic change occurred each year as the Passover season approached. Without any forewarning, without any explicable reason, an air of tension and apprehension permeated our home. Nothing was said, yet I felt an ominous foreboding. I knew that the tension was not directly related to the Passover but, rather, to Easter, which was celebrated at about the same time by our Christian neighbors.

Already before the festivals, at school, my Christian classmates refrained from playing with me, even uttering hostile remarks. Older children, on the street, would try to beat me up or pull my earlocks. The climax, however, was reached on the day of the Great Procession.

Early in the morning, hundreds of villagers and their families, both from Berek and from adjacent hamlets, would gather in front of the Greek Orthodox church bearing icons, flags, banners, and crucifixes. Following excited addresses by the priest and by some other dignitaries, the mass of people formed into columns and began marching, all the time uttering chants and lamentations in a language I did not comprehend.

No Jew would dare show himself in the street during the procession. We all remained at home, doors and shutters closed. In silence we watched the procession through window slits as it wound its way through our narrow street.

The event had never rationally been explained to me. Yet I felt that something awesome must have happened, which was remembered and reenacted year after year just as we were preparing to celebrate the Passover. We Jews were silent participants in this drama.

Not always, though, was our role passive. At times, when passions ran high, rocks would be thrown at our windows and abuse heaped on our homes. Once a child neglected to take shelter during the procession; he was pelted with rocks until he came running home, blood gushing down his cheeks.

As soon as the celebrations were over, the peasants returned to their homes and the evil spirits dissipated. Relations between Jew and gentile returned to normal, until next year same season. Could that be the reason why Jews exclaim on Passover night, "Next year in Jerusalem"?

During wintertime, our river was frozen and could not be used for immersion in honor of the Sabbath. For married women of reproductive age this presented a serious problem. According to Jewish religious practice, such a woman must immerse herself in a ritual bath, *mikveh* in Hebrew, following her monthly menstruation. Only after she has immersed herself may she resume marital relations with her husband. This practice was almost universally observed among Jews in prewar Europe.

Now the tiny Jewish community of Berek did have a mikveh, but it had fallen into disrepair. Since no funds were available for the restoration of the mikveh, the women of Berek had to travel to Szatmár for their monthly immersions.

Once, a member of the Jewish community of Berek died. In his will he left a certain amount of money for the express purpose of repairing the mikveh. His son, however, used up all of his father's funds on some unsuccessful venture. The mikveh remained unrepaired.

One early morning the village night watchman came to father and told him that while he was pacing the previous night in front of the deceased man's house, he had heard bitter shouts and pleadings coming from it. After a while, everything was quiet. Father did not attribute any special significance to the report. Besides, the night watchman used to get drunk at times; so father thought he just might have imagined what he had reported. When he brought a similar report the next day, father paid a visit to the widow. Following a short conversation, the widow told him that her deceased husband came to her every night and tried to suffocate her because she had not fulfilled his will concerning the repair of the mikveh.

Next day father assembled ten adult men, and together with the dead man's wife and son they all went to the cemetery. There, in front of the fresh grave, wrapped in their prayer shawls, the assembled men recited psalms and penitential prayers. Then father spoke directly to the dead man. First he asked his forgiveness that his will had not been fulfilled. Then he adjured him by authority of the assembled congregation not to disturb any more the peace of his wife. He charged him to abide in the domain of the departed and to desist from coming among the living. As the ceremony was still taking place, clouds covered the sky and a storm started to rage.

It was reported that following this dramatic event, about which the villagers would speak for years to come, the dead man no longer returned to his wife. No more strange sounds were heard by the night watch when pacing in front of the dead man's home.

In spite of the very small number of Jews that lived in Berek, life was not dull or monotonous. To begin with, there were lots of children—the families of the rabbi and the butcher alone provided twelve children. Our holidays were filled with joy, excitement, and anticipation. The several occasions when we could slip away to the river or to the Great Forest adequately compensated us for the tedious hours we had to spend at cheder. Nor were we unappreciative of the wisdom and values our teacher at cheder worked so hard to instill in us. Although, at times, reluctantly, we knew well our destiny and what was expected of us. Verses like "It is a tree of life to them that hold fast to it, and everyone that upholds it is happy," and similar verses that we heard at home and at synagogue, had not been lost on our young, impressionable minds. Besides, that was our way of life, and we knew no other.

One day, all this ended abruptly. Father told us he had decided that our family would move to Szatmár. The meager income that Berek's small community afforded him simply was not enough to make a living.

2

Spring Festivals

THE DAYS OF Purim and Pesach, and of the month in between, were a time of renewal. It was spring; we children quite ready for freedom, for a quickening of our winter-sapped spirits.

Purim commemorates the Jewish triumph over Haman. He had intended to massacre the Jews of Persia, but the Jewess Esther pleaded with her king to spare the Jewish people by negating the designs of his subordinate Haman, and the king did so.

On Purim, Jews are required to listen to the reading of the Megillah, the Scroll of Esther, which tells of her victory over Haman around 450 B.C.E.

In other places, at later times, for centuries without end, Jews have suffered death and destruction because of one whim or another. The Megillah of Esther and the observance of Purim came to signify hope.

When the Megillah is read in the synagogue, the reader articulates the text so carefully that not one word of the scroll goes unheard. At each mention of "Haman," children whir bull-roarers, adults stamp their feet upon the floor—all join in the "beating of Haman," the symbolic eradication of an evil person's name. Then quiet is restored, and the reading progresses.

About the time I was beginning to comprehend the events of Esther's story, a pitiable mensch named Hitler was moving toward the fulfillment of his infamous designs.

During the Purims of my adolescence, our noise was thunderous, the congregation virtually unrestrained. We heard each "Haman" and let loose our anger; we heard each "Esther" and let soar our pride.

In Purim tradition, collective hardship and humiliation, pent-up pain and anguish found a harmless outlet. Purim preserved a people in diaspora. Much more than a minor festival, it represents an ingenious and noble approach to the mental health of an entire nation.

Somewhere in time, the custom of carnival was added to the total of Purim observance. The wearing of mask and costume, the escape into merrymaking, was not only sanctioned, it was insisted upon. So we partied.

All year long one is required to wear a mask in order to comply with convention or expectations. On Purim, for at least a few hours, one is permitted to be his real self by taking on whatever disguise his heart desires.

Another custom pertaining to change of identity or role was followed in the greater yeshivot. An outstanding student would dress and act like the rabbi; he would even assume the rabbi's chair. Students would approach the festival rabbi with their personal problems; he would bless them and grant them promises of healing and salvation. When the official rabbi came in, the imposter was unmasked and banished from the chair.

As a child, I heard the story that once, when the official rabbi had taken his seat, his countenance instead of gaiety reflected gloom. His words to his students were thus:

"Your Purim prayers have been received in heaven in all serious-ness. The promises of your Purim rabbi have been granted, but what a pity! Your petitions were trivial and personal. Had one of you asked for the Redemption and the speedy coming of the Messiah, your request would have been answered. Now who knows how long the world shall suffer until another such hour presents itself?"

The days after Purim and before Pesach seemed to belong espe-cially to us children. The snows had melted and left in their place rivulets and puddles. We arrived at cheder with wet shoes and later stood before our mothers with shoes once again sodden.

It was spring, and even our cheder rabbi softened. We now studied the Pesach Haggadah, which is the order of celebration for Passover, and also *Shir HaShirim*, the Song of Songs. "For see, the winter is past, the rain is over and gone; the flowers have appeared on the earth, the time of song has come, and the call of the turtle dove is heard in our land."

While in winter we had not minded spending long hours confined in cheder, now we began to be impatient; expectation hung heavy upon our stuffy souls. A week or so before Passover, we would get our vacation. We would then have two weeks in which more fully to be children.

Even before vacation, we retrieved the treasures hidden away during the rest of the year. These were kept in cloth sacks or, lacking them, in socks.

And what were these our treasures? Apricot and prune pits.

When weather permitted, we gathered for a game of pits. We dug a small hole in the ground and then, from a designated distance, thumb-flipped our pits into the hole.

In a bag separate from the pits, we safeguarded our buttons. They were harder to come by and were, hence, more precious. Button values varied. Most coveted were the mother-of-pearl, then those of bone, next the wooden ones, and finally, tin. Not only their basic material, but their size and shape also determined values. Only "experts" could assess the point value of a button, and their verdict was accepted without challenge or doubt. Thus, button barter and exchange was in itself an attractive pastime.

Our button game was a variant of the pit toss. We drew a grid in soft earth or with chalk upon the pavement. Buttons were staked in the grid sections and then, thumb-flipping our button cache, we either increased or diminished our holdings.

I suppose I was no different than the other boys, for, wishing to augment my button collection, I more than once cut a button from coat, jacket, or shirt. To my mother I would simply say the button had fallen off, it was lost.

But surely the Holy One, praised be He, understood our frequent transitions from lies and gambling to pious study of the holy books, of the sacred traditions.

Back at the bench with the Passover Haggadah open in front of us, we delighted in the wondrous miracles the Almighty had performed on behalf of the Hebrews in Egypt, and we marveled at the afflictions visited upon the Egyptians.

What most fascinated me was the account of the ninth plague. When this punishment befell Egypt, people could not see one another; for three days no one could move from where he was. But all the Israelites enjoyed light and freedom in their dwellings.

What a God-sent situation! If I had been there, I would have gone to the home of my father's taskmaster, the one who made father's life so miserable. I would have called out the taskmaster's name from one direction, then from another, and still from another. Not only would he not be able to see me in the cloud of darkness, he would not even be able to turn his head in my direction! What torment I would have heaped upon him.

That accomplished, my mind returned to buttons. What kind did taskmasters wear on their garments? Crocodile bone? Gold, perhaps? Did the Hebrew children in the land of Goshen eat plums and apricots? Did they save the pits and hide them in small bags?

Mattress stuffing was another of the raptures of spring. The week before Passover, my brothers and I would empty the ticks, carry them to a nearby farm, and stuff them overfull with virgin straw.

On that first night, I would throw myself upon the pregnant tick, settle, then lovingly shape the mattress to my liking.

Gone, at least for a time, was straw compressed nearly to dust and nothingness, gone the agony of sleeping virtually upon board.

Once, some three days before Passover, when I was but six or seven, a keg was delivered to our home and placed upon the porch. The keg was left outside because to have brought it inside would have rendered it unfit for Passover use.

Mother was just then in the process of a thorough housecleaning as a preliminary to our traditional search for and removal of every crumb of *hametz*, or leavened bread.

When the children of Israel were standing by for word to leave Egypt, they could not wait upon leavening, and so they were commanded to have unleavened bread ready. They were commanded of the Lord God, "No leaven shall be found in your houses."

Thus, eating or even possessing a crumb of leavened bread is forbidden during Passover.

Not until all leaven had been removed from the house could the keg be taken inside.

Absorbed in her cleaning, mother did not even once come outside to note what her sons were doing. Besides, she had absolute faith in us; we would never do anything unbecoming. Indeed, we never would—had it not been for our neighbors, the butcher's sons.

Across the street from us loomed a tri-tiered, red-roofed house. In comparison to all the other houses in Berek, it was magnificent. It housed the Bergers, the village butcher family. Obviously, they were rich, and casual about their Jewishness. On the other hand, we were the rabbi's family, and not only was father the rabbi, he was the cantor and the ritual slaughterer as well. We were pious, ultra-Orthodox, and in no danger of becoming rich.

From among all the exotic furniture I saw at the Bergers, some of which had been imported from distant cities, I was most taken with the grand piano which possessed half a room.

The piano was Katzia's, and I was her devotee.

Aside from the chants and melodies of synagogue, I knew only the violins and songs of the Gypsies who entertained us at Purim and at weddings. Somehow, their violins brought to mind David, shepherd king of Israel. It is told that he would hang his harp near his bedside before he slept. Exactly at midnight, a northern wind would blow upon the harp, creating heavenly melodies. Awakened, King David would then rise, composing his psalms as the earth turned toward a new dawn.

My Gypsies and their violins were one thing, but Katzia and her music sounded to me no less divine than the wind upon David's harp. Katzia's family appeared to take her talent for granted, and so I alone would sit and listen, watching her beautiful fingers call forth music I otherwise could not have known.

I listened; in turn she plied me with cookies and candy, and when she would play no more I found time to join her younger brothers and my older ones.

Much that we did I cannot recall, but I remember that on Sabbath afternoons we would gather in the orchard adjacent to the Berger home. When the fruit ripened, our temptation was to pick an apricot, pear, or apple. Yet my brothers and I well understood that picking fruit was a violation of Sabbath law. But then we somehow determined that if picking with our hands was prohibited, picking with our teeth surely would not be. And thus we ate forbidden fruits, over the seasons conditioning ourselves for our ultimate shame, the keg incident.

There I stood, watching two of the butcher boys and two of my brothers examine the keg. They moved it around a bit; it was heavy, full. We tried to get a whiff of the contents and failed. The keg was neatly sealed, a bung at the top, buried in red wax. One of the butcher boys suggested opening the keg. We voiced no objections. So off he ran across the street to the butcher shop, returning with a very sharp, very narrow knife.

He began drilling into the seal; after some strenuous effort he made a fine hole not only through the wax but through the bung. A delicious fume came rolling out.

Now what? Their side had gotten the knife. The next step fell to us.

But we couldn't go into the house to get a pitcher or glasses; mother would surely spoil the whole project.

Then someone pointed to the backyard. There was no need for elaboration. Out back lay the excess straw from our mattress rejuvenation. We all raced to the back and returned with promising straws.

We took turns, one or two sips at a time. Nobody paid attention to the number of turns or to the length of time spent drinking; after all, stolen spirits are sweet.

One thing else is beyond doubt—we boys were found dead drunk wallowing in the mud. We had fallen into a ditch while chasing some storks in a nearby field that belonged to the village priest.

All day cleaning, and then mother had the fine task of washing her fallen angels and putting them to bed.

When Passover came, the Jewish community of Berek had to observe the festival without whiskey. Our tampering had rendered it unfit for Passover use.

For a long time afterwards I had felt shame and deep sorrow for the humiliation and pain we had brought upon our parents on that Passover eve.

I imagine that a fifth question circulated in Berek that year, in addition to the four traditional Seder questions. I suppose that not a few adults were asking, "And where should we store the Passover whiskey next year at this time?"

3

Fall Festivals

I WAS THE fourth among five brothers—Antshel, the oldest, and Shiele, the youngest, did not come back from Auschwitz.

To be fourth in line had certain drawbacks and disadvantages. When it came to clothing, for example, the younger child was usually given his older brother's worn-out wardrobe. Seldom did I get a new pair of shoes, a new hat, coat, or suit. My only consolation was that Shiele, being fifth in line, was even less fortunate than me in having a chance for some new article of dress.

On Rosh Hashanah and on Passover I would envy those of my friends who came to synagogue dressed in brand-new outfits. Our family struggled hard to make ends meet. It was difficult enough to feed seven people, pay the rent, heat the house in winter, and pay for cheder. Not infrequently I went to school in the morning on an empty stomach—there simply was no food at home.

My brothers and I felt that we must shoulder the burden and come up with some extra money. That was easier said than done. Opportunities to make extra money did not present themselves readily. Yet one such opportunity did come along just before Sukkot, the feast of Tabernacles, which occurs in the fall.

On Sukkot, tradition requires of the faithful to build a temporary dwelling called a sukkah and then to spend as much time as possible in the hut erected for the festival, and especially to have as many meals there as the weather permits.

Originally commemorating the huts the Israelites dwelt in during the forty years following the exodus, the sukkah also brings one into closer communion with the Almighty, impressing on him the precariousness of life and the vanity of earthly possessions. All of the parts of the sukkah are reusable year after year, except for its roof covering.

The sukkah covering constitutes the most essential part of the hut and must be fetched anew every year from the field or the meadow.

On the outskirts of our city, Szatmár, in the marshy areas beyond the forest, there lived a tribe of Gypsies. The Gypsies were a vivacious and lively people. Like the Jews, the Gypsies too produced great numbers of children. Like the Jews, they too used to exhibit merriment and optimism. From his early childhood the Gypsy would practice the fiddle, learning to produce pensive sounds. They would come with their violins and with their dancing skills to entertain us at weddings and on Purim. They used to claim that sometime, somewhere, in the dim historical past, their ancestors were related to the Jewish people; hence some of the similar traits in both peoples.

Before Rosh Hashanah, my older brothers would go to the Gypsies and negotiate the wholesale purchase of the reeds which grew in their marshes. The bargain struck, all five brothers would go out many times to the marshes from early morning till late into the night, to cut, gather, and tie the reeds into equal bundles. This completed, we would carry the fresh-smelling bundles to the synagogue square, where ultimately we would sell them to be used as roof thatching for Sukkot.

We took turns at sleeping in the square, guarding our merchandise. The nights were already cold; I shivered there in the open, but took delight at being away from my parents' eyes, as if I were on my own. I felt thrilled sleeping in the broad vistas under God's wide skies. I fancied the full expanse of the firmament as one great universal sukkah watched over by the Holy One, who in His infinite mercies was keeping a watchful eye even over me, one of His younger servants. How pleased He must have been to see one as young as I laboring so that hundreds could obtain reeds and perform the mitzvah of building a sukkah.

On Yom Kippur I fasted all day long, although not yet Bar Mitzvah. The atmosphere in our synagogue was so overwhelmingly charged with piety and penitential devotion that many children my age decided to fast. It was a feat of self-discipline that brought deep spiritual satisfaction.

Neither appointed rabbi nor professional cantor, the leader of the service at times managed to lead the worshippers into a trance of holy ecstasy.

From my childhood days I have carried with me vivid impressions of some of the highlights of the Yom Kippur service. No less than eight times, the entire congregation recited the Confessional. Without prodding or prosecutor, an entire congregation sobbingly pleaded guilty to crimes they had not only never committed but had never contemplated even in their remotest fantasies.

The opening statement set the mood.

> What can we say to You, what can we tell You? You know the mysteries of the universe, the secrets of everyone alive. You probe our innermost thoughts, You examine our thoughts and desires; nothing escapes You, nothing is hidden from You.

I loved the Neilah service of the Day of Atonement at dusk. I looked forward to the Closing Service with anticipation, not because it heralded the approaching end of the fast, but rather because, instead of the by now somewhat overworked confessions, it contained the following words, soothing and healing.

> You extend Your hand to transgressors, ready to embrace those who turn in repentance. You have taught us to confess all our sins to You, that we may cease doing violence to our lives. . . . You are gracious, compassionate, patient, and abounding in kindness.

Although legally the fast was over with the blast of the shofar and the resounding exclamation by the congregation of the immortal words "Next year in Jerusalem," we mastered some extra strength and willpower to stay a few extra minutes and join in the Blessing of the Moon.

If I were asked today which feature of the Yom Kippur service most profoundly shaped my abiding attachment to the destinies of my people, I would point to the two afternoon sections, the Avodah and the Martyrology.

Ever since the Second Temple in Jerusalem was destroyed by the Roman legions in the year 70 C.E., the awe-inspiring service conducted by the High Priest on the Day of Atonement in Temple days has been annually recounted in the synagogue. His solemn offerings, the sprinkling of the blood on the altar, his many ablutions, the changing of his colorful vestments, the designation of the scapegoat and its consignment into the wilderness. None of the details have been overlooked. The climax, however, is reached when the leader of the service, dressed all in white, recalls the ancient formula of Confession offered by the High Priest when secluded in the Holy of

Holies. Just like the High Priest in Temple days, our leader too would fully prostrate himself in front of the open ark, chanting in awe the ancient words: "And thus did he say: O God, I have committed iniquity, I have transgressed, I have sinned against You, I and my household. I beseech You, O God, to forgive the iniquities and the transgressions which I have committed against You, I, my household, and the children of Aaron, as it is written in the teaching of Moses: 'For on this day, atonement shall be made for you to cleanse you of all your sins."

It was then and there, secluded inside the Holy of Holies, engulfed by the smoke of the incense and in encounter with his Creator, that the High Priest pronounced the glorious ineffable Name of the God of Israel. The people and the priests upon hearing the echoes of the Name reaching them from the Holy of Holies, would bow and kneel. Falling with their faces to the ground, they responded: "Praised be His glorious sovereignty for ever and ever."

For us children watching this elaborate performance was tantamount to witnessing the original. The overpowering impression was deepened when, at the conclusion, the entire congregation chanted:

> In truth, how glorious was the high priest as he came forth from the Holy of Holies in perfect peace. As the iridescence of the rainbow in storm clouds . . . as the morning star shining in the border of the east was the countenance of the high priest. While the Temple was on its foundation, and when the high priest stood and ministered, his generation beheld and rejoiced.

For a moment, the congregation had been swept away to the distant glorious past, far away from the oppressive present, the agonizing realities. How comforting it was! How soothing! Yet a living and thriving community cannot dwell in the past. It must face the present, no matter how dismal. So the congregation continued its lament.

> Happy the eye that saw these things—the exaltation of Israel in the Sanctuary, the singers singing sweet songs, the high priest praying unto Thee, the scarlet fillet becoming white—to hear all this, verily, makes our souls sad.

Immediately following the Avodah service comes the section that so typically characterizes the history of the Jewish people, the Martyrology.

Although recorded Jewish martyrdom goes back to the first half of the second century B.C.E., the era of the Maccabean revolt against the Greeks, the Yom Kippur liturgy traces its martyrology to the first half of the second century C.E., some three hundred years later. Yet historical precision was not the decisive factor when father took me under his large tallit and chanted the names of the ten martyrs and the details of the tortures inflicted on them by their Roman executioners. It was the terrible reality that left its imprint on the mind of the impressionable youth.

The days between Yom Kippur and Sukkot were the busiest of the entire festival season. Immediately following the breaking of the fast, the reed market came alive. The three or four days of selling permitted before Sukkot were a marvel of competition and bargaining. Surely I shouted the loudest, offered the finest of Szatmár reeds. When I wasn't enticing customers, I was hauling. Home delivery was one way of nailing a buyer. Usually I was the one who made the delivery upon my shoulders. Although included in the deal, in most cases I would get a tip for this extra service.

The thrill and the excitement of the reed market were soon over. Lulav and ethrog purchased, our own sukkah was covered with the choicest of reeds and colorfully decorated. Decorating the sukkah was mother's domain. Her most exquisite creations were birds of many kinds, colors, and shapes, suspended from the ceiling, gently fluttering in the sukkah breeze. The birds, fashioned out of carefully emptied eggshells, were meant to impress on the sukkah dwellers the prophetic promise, "Like the birds that fly, even so will the Lord of Hosts shield Jerusalem, shielding and saving, protecting and rescuing."

Weather permitting, father made it a point to sleep in the sukkah. Shiele and I would take turns, as there was room only for one additional cot.

Upon returning from synagogue on the first night of Sukkot, we did not enter the house, but made our way into the sukkah, which now became our home for the next seven days. Mother had already lit the festival candles and placed at the center of the table wine for Kiddush, challot, and honey.

Seldom did I see father's face so flaming and excited as at the time when, upon entering the sukkah, he solemnly exclaimed: "I invite sublime guests to dinner. . . . O Abraham, my exalted guest, may it please you to have all the exalted guests dwell with us—Isaac, Jacob, Joseph, Moses, Aaron, and David."

While on Passover, at the Seder dinner, there is only one guest who visits Jewish homes, the prophet Elijah, on Sukkot there are seven. The extended invitation for them to join the family for dinner was more than mere lip service. A sense of their presence hovered in our sukkah as the solemn words were spoken.

The seventh day of Sukkot has an entity and a uniqueness of its own. It is Willow Day. Services begin quite early in the morning and are extensive. The main feature of the day is a bundle of five short willow branches held by the worshipper while the congregation is chanting a variety of Hoshanah prayers and hymns. Those branches whose leaves are without blemish, and the deep green color of which show some traces of pinkish shade, are the most sought after. Devout worshippers do not mind paying more generously if the right branches of Hoshanot are available.

On the night before Willow Day, I would take my sharp knife and a huge bucket, and go down to the banks of the Szamos River. Already weeks in advance I had visited the site to pick and carefully mark the places where the choicest willows were growing.

Knowing well there were only a few hours left, I unleashed all my energies in a cutting spree, and my bucket got ever fuller with lush, greenish-pink willows. Some of my fingers still bear testimony to the perfect performance of my knife.

A perfect, fully shaped moon and myriads of stars provided me with both light and companionship in my lonely, yet joyful, chore.

Around midnight I arrived home and immediately started sorting out the branches according to size, tied them into bundles of five, and left them in the water to preserve their freshness. There still remained a few hours of sleep before taking my willow bundles to the synagogue and exhibiting them in pride.

I would go first to the synagogue where services began very early. About half of my willows sold, I would then take the rest to our synagogue, where services started somewhat later. In a matter of minutes, all of my bundles were gone. All but one. The previous night, as soon as I returned from the river, I had picked the five choicest willow twigs, tied them into a neat bundle, and put it carefully away for my own use.

Inside the synagogue, merchant turned worshipper, my right hand tightly grasping the willows, I watched in fascination the seven Hosanna processions of the elders around the altar. Ethrog and Lulav in their hands, the holy ark open, they would implore "Hoshanah! Help, O God! Merciful God, please, help!"

It was the second procession that evoked the loudest exultation. It is entirely devoted to the eternal city of the Jewish people. The following epithets are telling.

> The world's Foundation Stone, the House of Thy Choice, Sacred Shrine, Hill of Revelation, Abode of Thy Majesty, Lovely Height, Joy of the Whole Earth, Perfection of Beauty, Lodging-place of Righteousness, Tranquil Habitation, Goal of the Tribes' Pilgrimage, Precious Cornerstone, the Excellent, Holy of Holies, Object of our Affection, Home of Thy Glory.

The climax of this unique service was reached when, following the seventh procession, the willow twigs were struck against the floor, shedding their leaves. It symbolically represented God's casting off of our sins, cleansing us from our transgressions.

The proceeds from both the reeds and the willows we turned over intact to mother, a welcome relief to the always scanty family budget.

The festival season was over. Reeds and willows were no longer merchantable goods. The auxiliary sources of income had dried up, while our family's needs before the approaching winter sharply increased. What next?

I decided to become a barber.

4

Barbering

NO, I DID not open up a barber shop. My entire equipment consisted of a simple wooden chair, a mechanical clipper, and a hand mirror. At the age of ten I became a mikveh barber. And why not? I cut hair for my father and brothers. Thus we saved money we never possessed, and soon I became skilled enough to earn some extra money for mother, so that her burden of providing for a family of seven would be lessened.

On Fridays I situated myself at the entrance to the mikveh where the Orthodox came for ritual purification prior to the arrival of the Sabbath. My work I considered a sacred calling, for the Jewish male is directed to keep shorn of hair, except for earlocks, in order to wear properly his head phylactery.

I never lacked for customers and soon established a reputation for the care I took in forming a perfect half-moon of hair at the top of the earlocks. Such a perfect circle not only conformed with tradition but looked best. My haircuts were so preferred that I worked for many hours, ending with a numbness in my fingers.

They waited, they talked; I cut hair and rejoiced when the little ones were brought to my care. They were my most cherished customers.

When a child reached the age of three, his father would bring him to the mikveh barber. Before the trembling lamb fully realized what was happening, his curly hair, except for the earlocks, had already fallen to the ground, leaving bare a skull never seen since infancy. All that remained from the youngster's hair was a curly earlock gracefully flowing down on each side of his forehead. At the hour of shearing, a deep transformation occurred within the child. The halo of white radiating from his shorn skull testified more than anything else that from now on he was to take things more seriously and to make his young shoulders available for the yoke of Torah.

19

From that moment forward, he was expected to wear, both day and night, a yarmulke, a skullcap, signifying that always the One above was watching, was watching over him. From that time onward, in the midst of slumber, he would startle, and, more asleep than awake, compulsively touch his head with both hands to feel whether his yarmulke was in the right place—on his head; then, reassured that his God kept vigil, he would sleep once more.

During my career as a mikveh barber I developed a keen perception of skulls, various colors and shades of hair, and the differences in their density. The conspicuous diversity in the locks dropping to the ground from beneath my clipper often made me wonder about the origins of these differences. I then remembered the rabbi at cheder telling us of Sennacherib the Assyrian, who conquered many peoples and dragged them away to other lands, thus causing great confusion among the nations. After Sennacherib, it was said, all the world's peoples had been mingled together in life, love, and character. This being so, I wanted to throw down my clippers, find the rabbi, and ask him what was the point of all the talk about racial purity that so gripped the attention of my elders during those most crucial years of the late thirties.

Yes; I considered my work as a mikveh barber a sacred calling, deriving from it as much pleasure as I did when turning the earned monies over to mother.

Yes; I loved those little children, those trembling lambs, so trustingly submitting to my clipper. I took special care not to pinch or scar their tender skulls.

Several years later, before they even reached the age of Bar Mitzvah, my lambs, those children, were gone.

5

On Geography

PUBLIC SCHOOL HAS always been a pain in the neck. I went to school only because not attending would have been a violation of the law and subject to a stiff penalty. In my extreme Orthodox environment, attending public school was considered a waste of time. Every available second was to be utilized for one single purpose—study of the holy books. Chummash with Rashi, the Talmud and its commentaries—the hairsplitting, endless give-and-take—books of ethical conduct, only these and their like were considered worthy to be accorded of the limited time allocated to an individual during his lifetime.

But is the study of languages, science, history, and geography considered mere idle talk, a waste of time? Do not these disciplines contain some inherent value of their own?

A disciple once posed a question to his rabbi: "Rabbi, is it permissible to engage in the study of Greek wisdom?" "Yes, my son," came the rabbi's soft answer, "there is no prohibition as such against the study of the wisdom of the gentiles. It is, however, simply a matter of time. The Bible enjoined upon us, 'Let not this Book of the Teaching cease from your lips, but recite it day and night, so that you may observe faithfully all that is written in it.' Now, my son," the rabbi concluded, "if you can find a time which is neither day nor night, in that time you may engage in the study of secular wisdom."

At six in the morning I was already sitting in front of my open Talmud volume trying to hammer out some fine point the rabbi had hinted at the day before. The early morning hours were considered free from distraction and, therefore, conducive to good concentration. Unlike the evening and afternoon hours, which were utilized for group study and discussion, the morning hours were devoted to individual contemplation. It was of the utmost importance that the young student develop a mind of his own, so that in time, following a few years of rigorous training, he would be able to make his own decisions and draw his independent findings, thus adding yet another brick to the ever-unfolding edifice of talmudic lore.

At eight o'clock I was at public school; a different language, different subjects, and other faces. Although I attended public school reluctantly, I loved the stories our teacher would read to the class at literature time. Indeed, my most favorite time at public school were the last twenty or thirty minutes before dismissal. In those minutes the teacher would read or tell a story to the class. When finished, she would ask: "Children, who would like to tell us the story of the Hidden Treasure?" My hand was the first to be raised high. As I looked around the classroom, there were few hands indicating a willingness to come forth and tell the class of the mysteries of the Hidden Treasure. When the teacher eventually called on me, the entire class sat spellbound as I took them along on a dangerous mission in a hunt for bat-infested caves in search of royal treasures deposited there by robbers many centuries ago.

Yes, I loved telling stories, as much as I enjoyed reading them. I was especially fascinated with giants and legendary heroes of far-away places and bygone times.

As much as I loved stories, I dreaded geography. The location of rivers, mountains, towns and villages, boundary lines, was my weakest point and my worst nightmare. The fact that I was the only Jewish boy in the class only exacerbated my dilemma. The teacher— by no means a philo-Semite—knowing that geography was my sore spot, would take special delight in calling me to the map, in front of the entire class, so as to expose my ignorance.

"Bernat, take the ruler, please, and point out to the class where the Siretul River merges with the Danube."

Before she even finished the last words of the sentence, all eyes had turned toward me. A sense of expectation pervaded every cubic inch of the classroom.

Slowly getting up from my seat, hands trembling, cold sweat girding my shrinking loins, I approached the huge map.

Before my eyes I clearly saw the river Jordan emerging from the Sea of Galilee, winding its way through the green and lush meadows of the Jordan Valley, encircling in its flow ancient palm trees whose tops reach out for the sun, finally descending into the Dead Sea never to emerge again.

This strange phenomenon had fascinated me ever since the rabbi at cheder told us that the Dead Sea is not only a big graveyard for all the fish and other small creatures whose ill fortune brings them face-to-face with this salty body, but that it is also the burial place for the river itself, which flows into it but never emerges from it.

Right there across the river was Mount Nebo, from the summit of which Moses, for the last time, viewed the Promised Land "from Gilead as far as Dan." My ears could still catch the echoes of the Eternal's thundering voice: "This is the land of which I swore to Abraham, Isaac, and Jacob, that I would give it to their descendents. I have allowed you to look upon it, but you shall not cross there."

Then, there, below the mountain slopes, stood the armies of Israel all poised and awaiting for the order of their new commander, Joshua, "Go and conquer!"

A loud noise of trumpet sounds and the crashing of walls was still lingering in the desert air, a faint echo of which reached my ears as I stood in front of the map, trembling and sweating.

Amidst the excitement and the tumult I heard someone calling my name.

"Bernat," the teacher's voice thundered impatiently, "are you daydreaming, or are you going to show the class where the Siretul joins the Danube?"

Her demanding tone brought me back to reality, yet not to full reality. Randomly pointing with the ruler at a spot on the map, I exclaimed: "This, I believe, is the point at which the Danube and the Siretul rivers merge."

There was a pause, silence; the entire class held its breath. Then, a sudden outburst of thundering and uproarious laughter shattered the deep silence. The teacher had a difficult time in restoring quiet and order.

6

Tishah b'Av

THROUGHOUT HISTORY SO many calamities have befallen the Jewish people that there is hardly a day on the Jewish calendar on which, at one time or another, some sort of misfortune has not struck at them.

Yet there are certain days which, in the words of the rabbis, were "destined for trouble." Tishah b'Av is certainly such a day.

Already three weeks before the advent of the ninth of Av, an air of pensiveness pervaded Jewish homes and the Jewish street. The somberness was not only felt but seen. Weddings and similar joyous activities would not be scheduled during those twenty-one days. Haircuts and shaving were not permitted. The last nine days of this three-week period witnessed heightened intensification of the somber mood, culminating in the twenty-four-hour fasting period of Tishah b'Av.

At cheder too there was a change of mood, a different spirit permeating our classroom. Our rabbi's looks softened, his voice mellowed. He became forbearing and forgiving. Certain actions of ours which on other days would elicit his ire now went unnoticed. Interestingly, we children responded in kind. We made an extra effort at better concentration in spite of the simmering heat. We tried hard not to cause our rabbi added grief or embarrassment. No doubt, the added subject matter of our studies had something to do with this change of mood.

During the "three weeks," the rabbi somewhat relaxed on the customary studies, concentrating instead on the woes, trials, and tribulations which befell the Jewish people during the destruction of both Temples, loss of independence.

"During these three weeks," the rabbi would address his young audience, "our people received more than their due share in the cup

24

of sorrows, which was not only filled to its brim, but overflowing."
He told us that all this started when our people was encamped in the
wilderness of Sinai and Moses sent twelve scouts to spy out the
Promised Land.

> At the end of forty days they came back from spying out the land. . . .
> They brought back a report and showed them the fruit of the land: "We
> reached the land to which you sent us, and it surely does flow with
> milk and honey. The people, however, who live in the land, are strong,
> and the cities are fortified and very large; and besides, we saw the
> giants there."

The rabbi sighed briefly and continued. "The whole trouble with
that generation," the rabbi told us, "was that they lacked simple
faith. Despite all the miracles on the sea and in the wilderness which
they themselves witnessed, they doubted God's promise to bring
them into the land."

From the distressful manner in which he spoke, there could have
been no doubt that he was referring to some sad event that had
occurred not many centuries ago, but yesterday or the day before. He
spoke of a tragedy that happened not to our ancestors, but to him and
to us, here and now. "Then the whole community lifted up their
voices and cried; the people wept that night." Our rabbi told us that
according to the ancient sources, that night was the one preceding
the ninth day of Av. When the Holy One, blessed be He, saw the
congregation of Israel mourning and weeping, He said in sorrow:
"This night you are mourning without reason; I pledge that in time
to come you shall have ample reason to mourn on this day."

Utilizing biblical and rabbinic sources, interspersed with his own
commentaries and insight, the rabbi created in our classroom a
situation of veritable reality. At times, we children did not see
ourselves as passive listeners, but rather as active participants in an
unfolding drama. Now we are on the Temple Mount; Titus's legionnaires are storming the citadel, butchering anyone who comes their
way. The confines of the Temple itself are ablaze. Priests, Levites,
and all others who had found shelter in the Sanctuary are now
leaping for safety amidst the consuming flames. A compelling sight
now captures our attention: Two elderly, white-bearded priests with
incense-offering implements in their hands are emerging from a
hitherto unnoticed chamber. They are followed by ten or twelve

white-robed, angel-faced child-priests carrying large keys in their hands. All peaceful, calm, and in no hurry, the two elderly priests are leading the bizarre procession toward a stairway. A Roman legionary, sword drawn, rushes in raging fury toward the children and their elders. His outstretched arm and sword remain suspended in the air to the shrill sound of his superior ordering him to desist. The procession, entirely oblivious of the incident, is climbing the stairway leading to a rooftop. Perplexed and awestruck, the legionnaires freeze in their places as they watch the strange event. Soon, the two priests and the children reach the rooftop. The two elders, holding up the incense-offering utensils, say: "Lord of the universe, since it is obvious that You did not favor but have rejected our offerings, we are now returning to You these holy vessels before the enemy comes and desecrates them." Then the two elders, with the holy vessels in their hands, leap into the flames. The children, upon seeing this, hold up their keys and say in a psalmodic voice: "Master of the universe, since You have rejected us from being the keepers of Your gates, and You have let the enemy come into them, we are returning You these keys You once had entrusted us with." Following the example of their elders, the children leap into the flames while chanting the daily hymn of the Temple service. A fiery hand descends from heaven and picks up the keys.

Not all of the stories our rabbi read to us or told us during the "three weeks" were related to the destruction. In order to strike a reasonable balance, he also engaged us in stories which bespoke the glory, the beauty, and the splendor of Jerusalem prior to its destruction. He enjoyed telling stories which recounted the unique wisdom of Jerusalem's young children.

Once a stranger encountered a child in Jerusalem's marketplace. He gave him a small coin and said to him: "Go and buy me some food of which I may eat my full and yet even more than what I have eaten will be left over." The child took the coin and soon returned with a bag of salt.

We wept over the fate of the priestly children who were consumed by fire, and we lamented those wise children of Jerusalem who were later devoured by the sword or by ravaging starvation.

On the eve of Tishah b'Av the children were exempt from cheder. Much before sunset, our family would gather for the final meal before the onset of the fast. It had to be concluded before sunset. The atmosphere at home was very heavy. Only necessities were spoken, and that too in a lowered voice and in brevity. It was as if a death had occurred in the family. The blessings over the food were pronounced in silence, and hard-boiled eggs were served, as was the custom at a meal after a funeral.

At synagogue the worshippers did not greet one another. Everyone seated himself on the floor or on low stools facing the holy ark, which had been stripped of its decorations. Lights dimmed, stifled sighs from the direction of the women's gallery piercing the heavy silence, the cantor burst forth in the traditional chant:

> Alas! Lonely sits the city once great with people! She that was great among nations is become like a widow.
>
> Bitterly she weeps in the night, her cheek wet with tears; There is none to comfort her of all her friends.

The sighs, moaning, and weeping now became intensified as the cantor proceeded with the dirge traditionally attributed to Jeremiah, an eyewitness to the tragedy. Men and women alike, an entire congregation was cleansing itself, clinging to the faintest of promises while reminiscing its tragic past, which was only a reflection of the dismal present.

> For these things do I weep, my eyes flow with tears: Far from me is any comforter who might revive my spirit. Zion spreads out her hands, she has no one to comfort her. I cried out to my friends, but they played me false.

Weeping and lamentation was now carried to and echoed from every nook and corner of the mournful synagogue. The stifled sighs in the women's gallery, now turned into open sobs, swept along the men too.

Yet even in the darkest of hours hope shines forth triumphantly. Jewish tradition condones no excesses, neither in joy nor in sorrow. In Jewish tradition, God Himself shares the grief of His people, as it is written: "In all their troubles He was troubled." And because of this unique intimacy with the Almighty, the promise of salvation is inherent in the very experience of grief. Thus, the congregation listened attentively and with deep relief as the cantor chanted:

This do I call to mind, therefore I have hope: The kindness of the Lord has not ended, His mercies are not spent; They are renewed every morning . . . therefore will I hope in Him.

On our way home, father took my hand in his, and we walked side by side silently. Yet the way he held my hand that night of Tishah b'Av conveyed more than words can. His looks and the touch of his hand were soothing, comforting, and reassuring.

Upon entering the house, father told me that in the messianic age Tishah b'Av would be celebrated as a joyous festival. He also told me that on the very day the Temple in Jerusalem had been destroyed, King Messiah was born.

7

The Circus Comes to Szatmár

THE NEWS SPREAD like fire in chaff. Clowns, boys, and old men bearing sandwich boards swarmed the streets, announcing aerialists and a gallery of freaks. Other clowns rode atop gaily festooned carriages, broadcasting more enticements through megaphones. The billboards of Szatmár sagged with circus folk and their smiles. And if all this were not enough to make a nine-year-old wish to become, just for a few hours, a loafer, an idler, maybe even an apostate, the same billboards promised elephants, lions, bears. The clowns, the magicians, the beast-wrestlers, and the trapeze swingers—all broadly smiled at Szatmár.

The only lion I knew was the one Samson had torn apart with his bare hands, as one would tear apart a kid, a young goat. That happened long ago and far away, in the vineyards of Timna. The rabbi who told us the story did so with eyes glittering, his lips atremble. In his voice we, the young students, could hear Samson's exultant shouts of triumph, and the poor cub's sighs of agony. But now I would see a real, live lion.

How I wanted to go to the circus. Yet I knew it would only cause me trouble and agony. Father was then away from home, but mother and especially my oldest brother would never give permission, not even if my going to the circus would somehow hasten the coming of the Messiah. Beasts, even though mentioned in the Bible, are, after all, unclean animals. Besides, they distract the mind from studying the Torah. To watch human beings wrestle with beasts merely for the fun of it was certainly unbecoming for a Jewish boy whose time ought to be dedicated to more worthwhile causes. I knew well that going to the circus was the epitome of frivolity and foolishness, the polar opposite of my ultra-Orthodox and circumscribed existence.

Yet I likewise knew I would be unable to overcome the seduction of the circus.

The commotion and the excitement created around the coming of the circus did, indeed, distract the children's minds from the holy books. Not only did our thoughts wander to the banks of the Szamos River even while our books were open in front of us, but we spent as much time as possible at the site where the circus entourage was encamped, raising tents, organizing for the opening day. As soon as cheder dismissed, my playmates charged off to the Szamos, jacket pockets stuffed with pieces of dry bread. When I found out what was going on, what could I do but follow?

The lions having not yet arrived, I proceeded directly to the bear cages. A piece of bread in my hand and trepidation in my heart, I shouted fervently *gura*, which in Romanian means "mouth." And when the beast opened wide its jaws, I tossed my crust of bread, electrified by the cavern which swallowed up my peace offering as the earth had swallowed up arrogant Korah and his followers, sending them into the pit of Sheol. Then, tired of the bear, we wandered about the camp, children of Israel in a strange, strange wilderness, delighted to be there.

And so things went until finally the day of circus arrived. I entered the tent of asininity, my admission pooled and loaned by errant cheder friends. It was fantasy, it was magic! The circus fired my spirit in a way altogether different from anything I had known in the past. While my fingertips picked and pulled at the hem of my jacket as if I were picking at the knotted fringe of my father's tallit, excitement superseded excitement. I was exhilarated, dizzy, fearful I might plummet headlong from the top row of the bleachers down into the sawdust and apple cores. Just as I became certain that I could withstand no more, drum and trumpet announced the grand finale.

Across the tent, and at the far end of the center aisle, the "high priest" was entering. The entire house rose, shouting, applauding. He wore a purple cape, adorned with medals and ribbons, and tights, his legs bulging at the seams. He bowed. The house went berserk, then suddenly silent. Down another aisle came two circus hands, leading the bread-loving bear with the big jaws to the center ring, where the beast was met by the purple-robed Goliath. Bear and man, they wrestled while we surged, deliciously aroused and tensed by every maneuver, every minute of that spectacle.

I had gone to the circus, sat now before the event I had most wanted to see, yet suffered the intrusions of my brother's voice:

> Thy servant kept his father's sheep; and when there came a lion, or a bear, and took a lamb from out of the flock, I went out after him, smote him, and delivered it out of his mouth; and when he arose against me, I caught him by his beard and smote him, and slew him. Thy servant smote both the lion and the bear; and this uncircumcised Philistine shall be as one of them, seeing he has taunted the armies of the living God.

But my brother did not come to challenge the bear-wrestler who had taken away a young lamb from the flock; yet I knew well he would certainly demand reckoning from me for having deserted the fold.

When I arrived home late in the evening, I did not lie. Everyone knew where I had been. It didn't matter that I was a child, given to a child's fancies; the punishment had already been decided upon while I was still enjoying myself at the circus. The penalty, by all standards, fitted the "crime," if not more.

8

Bible Stories (In Memoriam)

IN JEWISH SCRIPTURAL tradition, the Bible is arranged in three sections. The Torah, or Five Books of Moses, is considered the most holy. Designated Torah portions are studied during the week, then recited and chanted at Sabbath services.

The Nevi'im, or Prophets, beginning with the Book of Joshua and concluding with the Book of Malachi, is afforded a lesser measure of reverence. Consequently, the books of the Nevi'im have seldom been studied systematically, and knowledge in these books has often been quite shallow.

The books of the Ketuvim, or Writings, begin with Psalms and end with Chronicles. Of these writings, the Book of Psalms has received the highest degree of love and devotion. It has ever been the most enduring comfort for the Jews.

The psalms are divided into seven sections, one for each day of the week. Our reading and recitation of psalms was so frequent that most students had no difficulty in citing many chapters and verses by heart.

Thus, while my education in the Torah and in at least the Book of Psalms was ensured by tradition, my instruction in the prophets was surely something of an exception among cheder and yeshiva students. This exception was due to one of my first rabbis, my most dear and beloved teacher, the Vishever Melamed, Rabbi Yidl.

Although four decades have passed, I still remember, with affection and with awe, Rabbi Yidl, who introduced me to the leaders and champions of ancient Israel, and who created in me a love of Bible stories.

He had come to Szatmár from an impoverished hamlet in the Carpathian Mountains, from Lower Vishow. Dire poverty had driven him away from his family in search of sustenance. His only skills were the letters and pages of the holy books.

In Szatmár, a group of parents had joined together and hired Rabbi Yidl. Although themselves of modest means, these parents willingly assumed this financial burden so that their children might receive a quality Jewish education. Dozens of cheders existed in Szatmár, yet my parents and the others believed that Rabbi Yidl could do a more superb job.

He would receive his meals in turn at the homes of his students. Our cheder was a rented room; at night, it became the rabbi's lodgings. The furnishings consisted of a long, heavy table, two benches for the students, and a chair for our rabbi. There was also a sizable wall closet.

These arrangements disturbed me. Where did our rabbi sleep? There was no bed in the room, and the cupboard wasn't that large. Whenever I arrived at cheder early in the morning, he was already waiting for us, radiating a smile from the midst of mustache and beard.

One morning I happened to arrive before time. I found my rabbi removing blankets from our two benches pushed side by side. He folded his ragged coverings, returned them to the cupboard, and I helped him replace the benches for our class. He said nothing; I asked no questions.

We began cheder at six o'clock in the morning; by eight we older students were at public school until dismissal at noon. We were back at cheder by three o'clock, received a half-hour study break at 5:30, and then resumed our lessons from six until eight in the evening.

The main topics of study in Rabbi Yidl's cheder consisted of the weekly Torah portion, the writings of Rashi, and selected Talmud passages.

During our evening break, we ate the meager snacks carried from home. Ostensibly, this was our time-out, but Rabbi Yidl was strictly mindful of the words of Jeremiah, "Cursed be he who is slack in doing the Lord's work." He took most literally his sacred trust of our hearts and minds and could not, therefore, afford wasting even a single moment.

In retrospect, those thirty minutes must have posed a dilemma for Rabbi Yidl. He knew his young sheep needed to quiet their hunger, quench their thirst, break the tedium of a long, long day. On the other hand, he could not put aside Jeremiah's admonition. His solution was perfect; at least, I found it to be so. While we children ate, the rabbi read to us the exploits of Joshua, Deborah, Gideon, Samson, David.

The stories were captivating. Drawn and exhausted, our spirits suddenly took flight; we were born anew, just like the phoenix. The rabbi's countenance was transfigured; he radiated a special tenderness, a suggestion of otherworldliness.

When our story hour arrived, we washed our hands, recited the blessings, returned once more to our places around the table, and directed our eyes toward Rabbi Yidl. Like a general in charge of a special unit about to embark on a unique mission, he first assessed our alertness; then, pleased with our enthusiastic attentiveness, he would delve into the ancient deeds of valor, the miracles, and the dangerous missions.

I longed to have marched with Joshua, to have crossed the river Jordan when the waters were held back. I wished to have been by Joshua's side when the Lord God confounded the enemies of Israel.

I took courage from that great leader. I admired him for not having run from his foes, for having stood up in the defense of his people.

Mostly, the stories were about adults, about the men and women who directed Israel's entrance into that land flowing with milk and honey. I wondered about the children, about those like myself. How did they fare among the young Canaanites? Did the little Hebrews run away when taunted and molested, or did they know how to defend themselves?

In my mind, the stature of Joshua continued to grow, especially when one afternoon the rabbi told us, we who responded with mouths agape, that Joshua had command even over the sun and the moon.

The rabbi stopped, took a deep breath, looked at us to evaluate the impact of his words. Then, with heightened emphasis and with solemnity, he read: "O sun, stand over Gibeon! Move not, O moon, from Aijalon Valley!"

Excited and enraptured, he again stopped. Then in a lower and more relaxed tone, he concluded: "The sun stood still, the moon moved not, till the people had taken vengeance on their foes."

Rabbi Yidl was a natural teacher. When he read to us, time and place dropped away.

The people of the Bible loomed within us, alive and pulsating. We knew them in their greatness and in their weakness, we knew their struggles, defeats, and triumphs. We forged our identity through them.

Years later, when I was home from yeshiva for the holy days, I learned that Rabbi Yidl had died. Sleeping on benches with no mattress and inadequate blankets for too many cold winters had given the rabbi tuberculosis.

He had been a mighty warrior, no less than Joshua.

9

Midnight Vigil

OUTSIDE, FAR TO the west, the horizon was enveloped in flames. And while the rays of the conflagration sought every nook and corner of my humble room, already the palest of moons was rising over the rooftops, over the chimneys. In the solitude of my abode, and in the searching eyes of the longing youth, the redness of the sky's fringes presented a reality filled with mystery and awe. It was twilight. I wanted midnight.

I was a yeshiva student; one more hungry soul seeking sustenance.

Far into the night, I kept vigil, knowing that the Holy One, praised be He, sits at the beginning of each of night's three watches and roars like a lion, saying, "Woe to My children, woe to My people, whom I have exiled among the nations." And then, when darkness enshrouds the earth, just at the moment when midnight comes, the Holy One, blessed be He, sheds two boiling tears into the ocean, stirring the subterranean currents and raising great waves heavenward.

I was not more than six, perhaps seven, years old, when I could not fall asleep one night. Through my bedroom window, a huge moon, all full and complete, stared into my eyes. The more I looked at it, the more animated it seemed. I wanted to turn aside, yet my fascination with the moon wouldn't let me. Then, I heard faint sounds coming from father's room. I listened in bewilderment; he was uttering words and sobbing intermittently. When I opened the door, all shaking, my surprised father looked up at me from the floor, where he was sitting in one of his room's corners. His initial surprise over, father gently took my hand and seated me beside him on the floor. It was then that I heard for the first time of God's roaring like a lion, and of the two boiling tears He sheds into the ocean. That night's impressions would stay with me ever vivid, undimmed.

36

Six years later, away from home, sitting on the floor in a corner of my room, I was waiting. I was waiting for a sign that I had been remembered. I was listening for the shedding of those tears, until, at length, my heart grew faint. I felt compelled to rise from the floor, to rush into the deserted streets, to shout for my salvation, indeed, for the salvation of the whole world. Yet some power, stronger and more sublime than my desire, nailed me to the floor.

Then, in the midst of my anguish, I heard His voice, plaintive and sorrowful. "Once I had a palace, once a vineyard. Then came enemies and destroyed that palace, My Temple; they devastated My vineyard, Israel. Therefore, comfort Me; O comfort Me, My people Israel."

The time had come. I removed my shoes, spread ashes on my head, and chanting the Tikkun Chatzot, I cried out: "How long will there be crying in Zion, and wailing in Jerusalem? . . . Do Thou have compassion on Zion and rebuild the walls of Jerusalem. . . . Arise, have compassion, the cup of sorrows is overflowing."

I did as had my father and grandfathers before me. I asked the Holy One, blessed be He, for deliverance.

I felt great relief; I saw myself a partner of the Shechinah, the Holy Presence. Surely, my vigil had shortened the days of exile; surely, the days of Messiah were near at hand. My heart burst forth in gladness, burst forth and stopped.

From the pit of my stomach there rose a frightening whisper, a small voice, saying, "Crushed beneath all that pent-up sorrow, how burning must be His anguish, how searing must be His pain."

Midnight had slipped by, giving way to morning. I was thirteen, my world darkening with the loneliness of God, and with the sufferings of His people.

10

Yeshiva Bound

AT THE AGE of twelve, I was considered old enough to be sent off to a yeshiva (rabbinical academy). Szatmár, of course, was renowned for its yeshivas, but what would have been the point of remaining at home to study? How can one refine himself except by stepping out into a world more exacting?

All the days of my childhood had been but a prelude to this hour of departure.

We gathered there in our living room, Shiele, mother, father, myself. Shiele stood somewhat apart from us, looking down at his feet. With tears gracing her eyes, mother kissed me.

Looking directly into my eyes, father blessed me, once more counseled me to devote the best and greatest portions of my time and energy to study of the holy books.

"The things of the earth, my son, are transient and vain. What truly counts at the final reckoning is how many mitzvot you have performed and how much knowledge and wisdom you have accumulated."

He paused for a moment, took my right hand in both of his. Cautiously, he resumed.

"Beril, already you have studied nine years at cheder; still you are very young. This new life will not be easy. You will miss your family and friends. There will be temptations. Yet, if you always remember the blessings which the Holy One, praised be He, grants to His true servants, then you will not falter."

He stopped as if he had run out of words.

Father was a man of few words. Seldom did he engage in casual conversation. When he spoke, it was with purpose, each comment deliberately coined to convey only the essential. Anything more would be of no consequence.

I could sense his struggle. My father, who so often imparted volumes with the shrug of a shoulder, the wave of an arm, had something more to say. I stood waiting while he yet clasped my hand in his hands.

"Beril, all is lost unless you know priorities. What do you think is more important, study of Torah or performance of mitzvot?"

At that moment, I couldn't see how those two values could possibly be in opposition, so that one should be chosen above the other.

"I think they are equally important," was my reply.

"In a way, my son, you are right; yet the matter is not as simple as that."

Father was now gazing away from me, looking up at the ceiling as if better to concentrate on what next to say.

"The question is not new; our rabbis, of blessed memory, took it up. For two and a half years, they wrestled with the problem. Finally, they resolved it, concluding that the ultimate goal in life is performance of good deeds. Therefore, study of Torah is most important because it causes one to understand the nature of good deeds."

Convinced that his message had settled in my heart, father motioned that our words were at an end.

Both parents and Shiele walked with me to the bus station, and there I boarded the bus designated Míhályfalva, the town of Michael.

It was the first time I left home all alone, bound for an unknown place. There I would spend six months before returning home for Passover vacation.

All the other passengers were strangers; they talked about things which hardly made sense to me. I knew little of life outside my Orthodox community, but I could tell that most of them were peasants from the nearby villages, peasants who had earlier walked to Szatmár, laden with baskets of produce, some driving livestock before them. I could see that they had done their own shopping; so many bags and baskets filled with clothing, pans, small tools, and an infrequent toy jammed the seats and aisles that I had difficulty finding room even for my feet. The conductor had to sweat his way through the thick of the crowd and their belongings. The air was crammed with heavy, unpleasant odors.

As much as I tried, during that two-hour ride, to concentrate on father's directions for finding the synagogue, my thoughts kept returning me to Szatmár.

How does it look without me? Is Shiele sad now that he is all alone? He was four years younger, but we were close friends. He confided in me, respected me as his elder brother. Of his three older brothers he saw very little; they had left for yeshiva several years earlier. Who would tell him his favorite stories? I wanted to go back, to observe him just for one moment.

Of the five of us, Shiele was the most fragile and the most sensitive. Had mother burned up her energies with us four and the several miscarriages in between?

And mother, what was she doing now? Would she speak my name tonight at the table?

What had she thought when her second-youngest son also left her nest and went off? Would she now lavish all her love and attention on her youngest bird?

Mother was profoundly religious, even more rigorous than father. No room for compromise existed in her world view; no hardship was too heavy a price for the higher goals in life, for those values which transcended the here and now.

Early mornings I would see her praying silently so as not to awaken us. Then she prepared our meager breakfast and saw us off to cheder. In the evenings, long after we had gone to bed, she could be found sitting beside the kerosene lamp, mending socks, shirts, underwear, the mended parts often more extensive than the whole.

On Friday evenings before sunset, mother kindled seven lights, one for each family member. Standing before the burning candles, eyes shielded with the palms of her hands, she would utter prayers for our well-being. Sobbing, she would implore the Almighty to illuminate the eyes and minds of her sons with the light of Torah.

Candles lighted, blessing recited, prayers spoken, mother's countenance radiated peace and serenity. This change from solemnity to rapture was most heightened when all her sons were present at the Sabbath table.

On Sabbath afternoon she would read, in Yiddish, the weekly portion of the Pentateuch, embellished with scores of ethical parables and homilies. This concluded, she would read from *Menorat Hamaor*, the "Illuminating Menorah," written by Rabbi Yitzchak Aboab, a fourteenth-century authority on piety and ethics.

At times, mother would call me and read to me a passage, a parable, an exhortation she had found especially meaningful. Often she would add some insight of her own. I knew she wished to instill in me wisdom and piety, that to her mind only such ethical books were deserving of her son's time and attention.

When three stars appeared on the horizon, the Sabbath day drew to a close, and then mother again became restless and pensive. Silently she offered prayers to the God of Abraham, Isaac, and Jacob, imploring Him to shield and protect her sons and her husband during the six days of toil, to protect them from harm, humiliation, and suffering.

My thread of thought was abruptly severed by a harsh blast and the grating halt of our bus. A young boy was herding sheep across the road; grimacing, the bus driver had no choice but to wait. His crossing completed, the shepherd, smiling and victorious, glanced back at the driver.

We moved forward again; shortly the driver announced, "Final destination—utólsó álomás."

No one greeted me at Mihályfalva. I had never visited there, didn't know a single soul. Nonetheless, I wasn't too worried. I knew the procedures.

My bus had arrived just before eventide, the time when Jews gather in their synagogues for the Minchah and Maariv prayers. Father had given me a detailed route to a specific synagogue, but, my sense of direction being what it is, I managed twice to stray from my path.

Nor was the way easy even when I went where directed. In contrast to Szatmár, most of the streets of Mihályfalva were unpaved. I slogged through deep sand, grateful that my grip was small, containing only my prayer book and a few changes of clothing.

At last, I stood before my synagogue. I had walked in sand for maybe thirty minutes, couldn't imagine how the children of Israel had endured the desert all those years.

First removing my shoes to pour back the sands of Mihályfalva, then straightening my yarmulke, I went in for prayers.

11

Days and Demons

I WAS ALONE in Mihályfalva, at peace in the knowledge that my people would provide for me as their circumstances permitted.

So sacred a mitzvah is the study of Jewish law, wisdom, and tradition that all Jews are asked to support those who study. While the student's parents, if possible, paid their son's rent, the community was expected to support financially the yeshiva itself, and households to aid students individually by providing meals. At the beginning of each yeshiva term, Jews who could do so offered "days," meals at their tables.

However, it was up to each student to secure his own sponsors, his days. If he couldn't obtain a meal for Thursday, well then Thursdays didn't exist and he probably went hungry. Not a few students went through the term with an uncomfortable number of dayless days. Sponsoring a student was a mitzvah, but if it was a struggle for you to feed your own family, how much could you spare for others? Thus, the number of days available never matched student needs.

In spite of this lack, veteran yeshiva students helped the new ones classify sponsors. Some households preferred the young, others wished a student with a beard, testimony to stability and earnestness. Some liked lively students, others quiet.

Deciding I could be lively where necessary and quiet as needed, I took the sponsor list and went out to seek meals. For hours I trudged all over town, forth and back, sometimes in circles, knocking on strange doors. A number of times I was just too late. Other times, try as I might to appear otherwise, I looked too much as if not even the entire fish and half of the carrots would satisfy my appetite.

At last, the sun was going down; I could quit.

After sixteen stops, I had gained five meals. I considered myself a grand success.

During that first term, Wednesday was my best day as far as

friendship and quality of meals went. The beadle and his wife, a childless couple about fifty years old, treated me as if I were their own. Obviously, they delighted in providing for one whose toil was in Torah.

As for me, I would choose to fast, and later in the term often did, rather than go after dark to the beadle's house for supper.

While still at cheder, I had developed a propensity for reading and telling stories of demons, evil spirits, the wandering dead. What a host of odd beings flitted about, jamming Eastern Europe; some belonged to local folk traditions and superstitions, others equally troublesome were Jewish in origin.

If one cut his finger while slicing bread, a demon had pushed his hand under the knife. If one turned his ankle upon a stone, within that stone resided Asmodai. A stillborn child or an infant lost soon after birth had been stolen away by Lilith. Come misfortune or disaster, the demons or the dead had been at work.

Exactly at midnight, when the world turns topsy-turvy and the cock crows at the moon's disappearance, graves open. Myriad souls wrapped in shrouds and prayer shawls leave their rest and march to the synagogue, where they turn on all the lights to announce their presence. They come to atone for not having studied Torah while among the living. Some are commanded to study for thirty years, others for seven, still fewer for twelve months, but each according to the severity of his neglect.

The holy ark is opened, a scroll taken out. Each of the dead takes his turn at reading, learning what he should have learned long before.

Were that the end of things, it would be a fine retribution.

Trouble is, the living are not necessarily exempt from this gathering. Should some poor soul be wandering near the synagogue just at this hour, he would hear his name called. Powerless, he would soon find himself behind the bimah, reading aloud with the dead.

Rumors say that he will not live out the year.

I loved to worry my cheder friends with such tales. But, would you suppose that, the more I told and retold these stories, the more I myself became possessed by them?

Long days were no problem; I had my supper at the beadle's while the sun yet shone. When the cycle of seasons drew to its close, Wednesday's meal became a nightmare. I fasted, I stayed in my lodgings. I pretended to be sick, I forgot what day it was.

The beadle lived somewhat remotely from other houses, he lived in back of the synagogue. There was absolutely no way to get to his house except to pass by the synagogue's southern wall.

Although the dead were not wont to arrive before midnight, what if they should miscalculate or, may it never happen, decide to change the time?

I was terrified at the thought of hearing my name, wondered if I'd be called up to read Torah or spirit legends.

I struggled through one winter, not once mentioning my fears to my beloved benefactors. When the time came to renew old sponsors and obtain new ones, I did not return to the beadle and his wife.

I still wonder what they thought.

12

Yeshiva Routine

THE ROUTINE AT the yeshiva was as I had expected.

Three Talmud pages per week including some of the less difficult commentaries was the norm for the younger student. The more advanced were expected to tackle the more exacting commentaries. The older students would help the younger ones study. Everyone would analyze, dissect, and examine to the utmost of his experience and natural talents.

All week long, from early morning to late at night, we studied, taking only four to six hours of sleep. On Thursday especially, many would stay up until midnight or later to finish up a difficult passage, to clarify some intricate point of law or conduct.

Early Friday morning the rabbi would question our understanding. It was only a formality, however. No student ever took a chance but went beyond offering what was a perfectly defensible answer. To waver in the presence of the rabbi and the entire student body would have been devastating.

Friday mornings were the highlight and culmination of a week's labor. Then, concentration of mind and agonizing of soul received due recognition. Then, the individual was given the coveted opportunity to demonstrate his skill at smoothly sailing in the rough waters of the Talmud. Often, the student was afforded no more than two or three minutes in which he was expected to condense the essence of long and arduous hours.

The rabbi, face aglow, eyes bespeaking deep satisfaction, would interject here and there some new point of view, some new twist of logic in the hairsplitting give-and-take that had not come to our attention even during our best efforts. Sometimes it happened that one of the foremost students challenged the rabbi's point of view, offering his own hairsplitting arguments to prove his point. The rabbi then would quote new sources and commentaries in order to fortify his position. Some more elite students would take sides with this or the other contender. The younger students would watch in rapt adoration, a demonstration for them of how deep and multifaceted the words of the Torah are.

All in all, Fridays were calming, soothing, and rewarding. The rigid discipline of the week relaxed; the atmosphere softened and mellowed. Expectation permeated the air. It was soon to be Shabbat.

Morning recitations over, by no means did the yeshiva student go around idly, just waiting for the arrival of Queen of Days, the Shabbat.

The weekly portion of Scripture to be read in the synagogue on Saturday morning had to be reviewed three times on Friday, first in Hebrew, then in Aramaic, and then again in Hebrew. As Hebrew was the original language of the Scriptures, the Hebrew was chanted first. The Aramaic reading was next because once, long ago, that had been the language common to most Jews. Finally, a second Hebrew reading was given to show that the Aramaic was not considered equivalent to the sacred Hebrew.

Our task, however, was not confined to the three readings of the text. Our purpose was to approach a grander measure of the wisdom of Israel. In order for each student to gain deeper insight, he would turn to the commentaries of the masters of the Chassidic and Mussar traditions. In their writings, the searching student could find explanations and guidelines to the hidden meanings of every word, letter, even dot. Each commentary was an attempt to expand knowledge and to instill a sacred dimension into the world view of the adolescent yeshiva student.

The prophet Jeremiah stated: "Behold, My word is like fire, declares the Lord, and like a hammer that shatters rock!"

In response, the rabbis maintained that there are as many ways to interpret the word of God as there are sparks in a fire and splinters produced by a rock struck with a hammer, each interpretation representing one aspect, one spark of the ultimate truth inherent in Him.

In the afternoon the students went to the mikveh to immerse themselves in water in honor of the approaching Shabbat. Then, purified and cleansed, we flocked to the synagogue even before services began.

Enchantment radiated throughout the sanctuary. The truly pious gathered just prior to the Friday evening services for the traditional chanting of *Shir HaShirim*, the Song of Songs. We stood as if before the Holy of Holies voicing a chant that recalled the levitical singing of the Temple era.

Nonetheless, this song in which we so delighted was known to have been in olden days a subject of dispute. One point of view considered the *Shir HaShirim* scroll simply a collection of passionate love songs that should never have received inclusion in the canon of Holy Scripture.

> Behold, thou art fair, my love, behold, thou art fair.
> Your eyes are like doves behind your veil.
> Your cheeks are comely with circlets, your neck with beads.
> Your lips are like a crimson thread,
> Your mouth is lovely.
> Your breasts are like two fawns browsing among the lilies.

An alternative thought held that the Song of Songs was an allegory of God's love for Israel, and the two breasts, but an allusion to the two tablets of the law. Rabbi Akiva, shepherd, spouse, scholar, boldly proclaimed: "The world has never been as worthy as in the day when *Shir HaShirim* was given to Israel. For in it the Holy One, praised be He, praises Israel and says to them, 'Behold, thou art fair, my love, behold, thou art fair.' If all Scripture is holy," concluded Rabbi Akiva, "*Shir HaShirim* is the Holy of Holies."

Suddenly, there was abrupt silence. The rabbi entered, dressed in his colorful royal attire. Turning their attention toward the leader who was radiating warmth and solemnity, the worshipers soon split in two sections so as to form a path for the rabbi. The Shabbat service was under way, the melodies lifting our hearts no less than the candles burning in front of the holy ark.

13

Elisha or Akiva?

THE MOST PRODUCTIVE time for study, no doubt, was early morning, beginning at five o'clock. Then, everything was still, there were no external distractions. These were the hours best suited for serious meditation and contemplation. While the world slept, my friends and I probed Talmud.

Places which had survived only in name, preserved on the pages of the Talmud, assumed a reality more vital than the streets we had walked just hours before. Within these pages, rabbis who taught centuries ago in far-off Babylonia quickened before our eyes.

Here was the overstrict Shammai, whose impatience had long been a byword. I saw him glowering at his disciples when they showed even the slightest sign of fatigue. I heard him thundering, "Is not the Torah a fountain of waters restoring the weary?" And then, here was this same man saying, ". . . and receive all people with a cheerful countenance."

But it was Rabbi Meir who claimed my admiration more than any other rabbi. To keep the attention of his disciples during arduous expositions of the law, he would interject short moral lessons.

One day, when he could see that his followers's concentration had been strained to the limit, he abruptly changed the subject, asking, "What was Hosea's meaning when he says of the Lord, 'I will heal their backsliding; generously will I take them back in love, for My anger has turned away from him'?"

Like a cool breeze, this comfort and this challenge flowed over Rabbi Meir's students, lifting their sullen spirits. But he was in no hurry for a response. Gazing toward the far edge of his vineyard, wherein they sat, he waited for all to be awakened by the deep silence. Then he himself answered his question.

"By this, Scripture intended to say that the act of repentance is so beloved by the Holy One, praised be He, that even if only one person repents his sins, those of the entire world are forgiven."

I knew the prophet Ezekiel had taught that the penitent attains salvation for himself only, not for the entire world, not even for his own son. This particular morning I pondered why Rabbi Meir had spoken so emphatically on the virtue of repentance, elevating it to universal significance.

Might it have been because Rabbi Meir was a descendant of heathen proselytes who had embraced Judaism? Or was it because he was pained by a dangerous trend to apostasy among the cream of Jewish youth? Hadn't even his own beloved rabbi, Elisha ben Avuya, lost faith? Wasn't the world in turmoil, so that Ezekiel's dictum was no longer responsive enough?

Hadrian had just marked his victory over the rebel bands of Bar-Kokhba. Jerusalem lay in ruins, the surrounding countryside ran with blood; thousands of martyr corpses lay rotting in the fields.

Some of the formerly pious had found it convincing or advantageous to join the fledgling faith of the followers of Jesus of Nazareth.

Seeing the Judaism of Rabbi Meir's time threatened with dissolution, assailed from without and within, I then understood why he had so stressed the importance of even one single return to the fold.

I was deeply moved by the sacred zeal of Rabbi Meir to save Judaism at one of its most fateful crossroads. This rabbi, a student of both Elisha ben Avuya and Akiva, demanded of himself and of his disciples absolute and unflinching faith in the God of Israel, even when His dealings with His people remain inexplicable. No one should turn away or, having strayed, fail to turn back.

I thought about apostasy.

How could Elisha ben Avuya, such a giant in Judaism, such a master of the law, renounce his faith? Was it because so many of his fellows had suffered gross torture, severe mutilation? Because having seen a dog pick up and carry away the discarded tongue of Rabbi Juda, he, Elisha, lamented, "The mouth that uttered pearls now licks the dust! Is this the Torah and this its reward?" Was that the circumstance that caused him to cast aside his faith?

But then, how could Rabbi Akiva joyously sound God's name in the midst of the excruciating agony of the flesh hooks pulled by the Romans? How could he still at that moment say to his horrified disciples, "All my life I have asked myself, shall I be able to fulfill the injunction 'with all your soul'? Now that I am confronted with that injunction, should I falter?"

Elisha faltered; Akiva did not. I found myself posing a question not even angels might answer: Wherein lies the abysmal difference between the steadfastness of men?

I shuddered. Would my own rabbi ever renounce his faith?

Certainly not! Didn't he take repeated and special pains to impress upon us, his trusting disciples, the supreme command to sanctify God under even the most extreme circumstances?

Then, the inevitable query: How would I behave should my hour of trial arise?

I sank to the floor, praying God I never be put to such a test.

14

The Evil Inclination

STUDYING OUR ASSIGNED Talmud pages and commentaries consumed the bulk of my time. Yet I found no abiding fulfillment in hairsplitting legal arguments, in all that grinding, grinding over a kernel of wheat fallen into the soup. I knew even during my first years that I was already a good student, and I knew, instinctively but not in words, that I wanted something more, something for my soul, something intimate, mysterious.

From my study of Talmud itself I had noted that not all the great masters limited their thoughts to this dry business of crystallizing the law. Indeed, some labored unceasingly toward moral perfection. These were the pious and the saintly, those who believed that knowledge and observance of the law was only the least expected, the minimum required of the faithful.

For you see, the law, as presented in rabbinical teachings, makes concessions to human weaknesses and errors. Therefore, those who seek a special closeness to God and a cleaving to His Shechinah must strive for a higher virtue, must work hard to live more righteously.

The psalmist recorded that "the fear of the Lord is the beginning of wisdom." Later, the pious Rabbi Phinehas ben Yair gave fuller expression to this view, formulating the classic "ladder of saintliness."

The knowledge of Torah leads to watchfulness; watchfulness leads to zeal, zeal to cleanness, cleanness to abstinence; abstinence leads to purity, purity to saintliness, saintliness to humility, humility to the fear of sin; and the fear of sin leads to holiness.

This was the teacher, this the message for which I longed. This rabbi who placed holiness at the top of one's aspirations opened for me broad vistas more satisfying and more exciting than the routine Talmud.

To be sure, Talmud still took precedence. There was no question in my mind that I had to be fully ready for Friday mornings. Still, I developed a passion for books of the Mussar type. While such books insist upon scrupulous fidelity to the law, their main emphasis is refinement of thought, ethical perfection, piety, holy ecstasy.

In those books I absorbed in detail how to combat Satan and his agent, the Evil Inclination. I read in those books that human predispositions to err are legion, that the deceits through which Satan ensnares his victims are without number.

Far from being bold, the Evil Inclination moves cautiously, selectively. Cunning and relentless, he makes his victim yield slowly, step by step. Should the victim at length catch note of his own heartfelt suspicions, his awareness is nonetheless futile, his entrapment final. He has already fallen prey to Satan.

Therefore, the safest conduct is never to compromise, never to yield, not even in the slightest. The sacred Mussar books cautioned me against pride, vainglory, jealously. I was counseled to be absolutely truthful in thought as well as in speech.

Those admonitions, and others, I imagined I understood and could guard against. I was to be watchful at all times, day and night. Yes, even during one's sleep, the Evil Inclination does his dirty tricks.

Nothing in my first efforts toward piety caused me more anxiety than my adolescent sexuality. Not only was this phenomenon a wonder and a terror in itself, I was also utterly convinced that, whatever those feelings were, they surely offered the greatest foothold for the Evil Inclination. The more my sexuality manifested itself, the further I receded from God, or so it seemed at the time.

Without ever having received the least bit of specific information about human sexuality, I heard and read the usual counsel about erecting a fence within a fence, about creating double measures of self-protection and piety. For eons, the Jewish male had been cautioned that the eyes and ears were agents of sin; simply to look upon a woman, or to hear her singing, was conducive to impure thoughts. In my youth, I was even warned against looking at dresses strung on a clothesline.

For their part, the daughters of Israel were to dress modestly and to conduct themselves with chastity; they were not to arouse undesirable passions in the male.

I was given such an excess of caution that my interest in the feminine intensified, while my fear for my soul magnified correspondingly. If only there had been someone with whom I might have talked, shared my searing doubts, the unrelenting pangs. But this was out of the question; such topics were not to be openly mentioned.

Even as I conversed with my best friend, this issue was left lingering at the edge of my mind, was never touched with my lips. I needed desperately to know whether my yeshiva friend was also, like me, plagued by the Evil Inclination.

My comfort was the holy books. Only there could I seek solace and advice, know moments of triumph and exultation. Those times when I knew defeat and despondency in spite of the holy books, I thought of father and of his comment, "There will be other temptations too, my son."

The hour was midnight, or later. Not long before, I had concluded an extremely difficult lesson, which had been exhausting my mind for several days. Now I had succeeded in piercing what at first had appeared impenetrable. I was elated.

In this condition, I concluded my study routine with my daily ethical reading in the *Sefer Chassidim*, the "Book of the Pious."

I heard singing.

It sounded female, vaguely recognizable. I concentrated, asked myself, whose voice? Finally, I thought it to be the voice of Channah, very deep, soft. Then the quality changed, became high and thin; I now heard Rachel. No, again I had been misled. The voice sounded more like that of Tsiporah; tempting, lovely, it threatened to displace every bit of breath in my lungs.

Still, I was mistaken. The song belonged neither to Channah nor Rachel nor even to Tsiporah. All three were singing. Only the angelic chorus descanting morning hymns to the Holy One, praised be He, might have caroled more sweetly.

Their singing grew ever more intense. I heard the words clearly:

I am only a wildflower in Sharon,
A lily in a mountain valley. . . .
Like an apple tree among trees of the forest,
So is my beloved among the youths.
Under his shadow I love to lie, tasting his sweet fruit.

Enraptured, I listened. The words were familiar, achingly familiar, the expression of them such as I had never before heard nor endured. I made a supreme effort of concentration to find out where I was, to identify, to recollect. My thoughts were abruptly cut off by a new outpouring of even sweeter music, dazzling, intoxicating.

> He has brought me to his chamber of joy
> Hung over with love . . .
> His left hand is under my head,
> And his right hand caresses me.

I focused all my strength; I wanted to run, to run far, far from the voices, far from the song. I blocked my ears with my hands and ran. My feet were heavy, too heavy. A strong wind assailed my face, making running nearly impossible. The heavenly music rushed at me from all directions, overwhelming, overpowering. I ran, fell to the ground, got up, and kept on running.

I entered a valley of apple trees in full blossom. The blooms were of many colors, each emitting a scent of a different variety. The fragrant scents carried by the breeze filled my nostrils and lungs to intoxication. I breathed ever deeper to inhale the heavenly aroma that seemed to emanate from the very bosom of the universe.

Then, the horizon became filled with thousands of clotheslines drawn between the apple trees, hung full with dresses of every hue, size, and shape, all blocking my way.

They were still wet. Flouncing in the wind, they struck my face, knocking me to the ground. Exhausted, wet-faced, heavy-footed, I kept on running.

Suddenly, there before me lay open the gaping abyss, deep and wide. I couldn't stop. I screamed.

At the last moment, I grabbed a clothesline, hung suspended over the abyss, swinging in the breeze. A sensation of relaxation, of sublime pleasure, permeated my entire being.

In the morning I went to the mikveh.

15

More on Ghosts and Demons

ON ONE OF those interminable and oppressive summer days, when the air becomes as heavy as lead and dense vapors hover about the horizon, a secret was revealed to me.

It was at cheder, evening dismissal half an hour away, our drained rabbi asleep on the table. He snored; we ceased studying and began whispering among ourselves.

Peretz, my freckled friend, always active like a boiling pot, asked me whether I had already seen Mendel the madman. I was dumbfounded; did such people really exist? In Szatmár? In response, I simply shook my head, fearing Peretz would hear my heart pounding.

"Then come with me after cheder and you can look at him."

"What does he do?"

"Come and see."

"Where, where is he?"

"At home, but he won't come out. He's locked up in his room, and all his windows have bars."

"How big is he?"

"Not so big."

And then I learned that Mendel had been mad for ten years, for almost as long as I myself had been alive. And when I asked whether Mendel had been locked up all that time, Peretz told me that Mendel had been shut away only after he nearly strangled a child who had been tormenting him.

That piece of knowledge aggravated my curiosity as it hardened my fears. I imagined a Mendel breaking the bars, running berserk, jumping on me, and trying to strangle me. After all, weren't the insane endowed with supernatural powers?

55

We children could no longer contain ourselves. Our whispers mounted to subdued anarchy, and that, in turn, erupted into open restlessness. Yet all this left the rabbi unmoved, undisturbed. He was sound asleep, roaming the hills of Jerusalem, while our aching backsides knew it to be eight o'clock, the dismissal hour.

Much, much earlier, the rabbi's wife had brought him a glass of milk. By now emptied of its milk, the glass was standing near the table edge, three or four flies strolling around in it.

A student, slowly and imperceptibly, pushed a book along the table in the direction of the glass. Following several measured shoves, the glass fell to the floor, neatly exploding.

"What happened, what happened?" Looking around and at the floor, our awakening rabbi asked, "Who broke the glass?"

We, of course, were reciting, our voices muting his. "Who broke the glass?" he now shouted. This time, our mischievous one replied, "Rabbi, a black cat jumped over the table, knocking the glass down."

"A cat, a black cat?" He frowned, thought for a bit. "Perhaps a banished soul was reincarnated into this unclean creature. The sweet sounds of children's Torah study may entitle it to redemption and a place in heaven." Looking again towards the floor and the shards and splinters, he muttered, "But why should it break the glass?"

Black cat or not, we, the cheder children, surely found salvation; the rabbi dismissed us, sending us running to our various destinations.

Mendel was pacing his room forth and back, gibbering. While Peretz and I gaped through the window, Mendel alternately stared at us and then apparently ignored us altogether.

He had a long, reddish beard and thick earlocks. To my wonderment, they were perfectly curled. Who did this for him? His mother? He wore a splendid striped caftan, like those worn by certain sects of mystic Chassidim.

Had he gone mad because he had dared Pardes, the secret garden of mysticism?

It is said that the hidden teachings are not for everyone. An unwise, unguided attempt at knowing the deeper meaning of existence can easily lead to destruction and chaos, to the opposite of the hoped-for wellsprings of life and joy.

The Talmud relates that four disciples entered Pardes, the mystical orchard. The first looked and went mad, the second died, the third became a heretic and denied his faith. Only one entered in peace and left in peace.

Peretz was nudging my elbow, wanting to leave. I had seen Mendel; now on my way home I would hear his story.

He had been a brilliant yeshiva student. One evening he and a group of friends had been discussing the matter of souls emerging from their graves at midnight. Some believed, some expressed doubt. Mendel unequivocally expressed disbelief. "The dead are dead," he would say, "and there is no reason whatsoever for them to climb out of their graves."

But he was not left in peace with his point of view. The subject came up repeatedly, eliciting heated controversy, but never came to a decisive conclusion. Until one night it happened.

One of the older and more serious students, who up to now had been a silent listener, spoke up. He challenged Mendel to go to the cemetery at midnight and touch the newest grave. By so doing, the speaker suggested, Mendel would put to rest once and for all the futile controversy on ghosts and souls. According to the plan, Mendel was to leave his challenger's worn-out and disqualified phylacteries upon the grave of Shlomo, a friend buried three days previously. He was to go to the cemetery that very midnight, place the phylacteries on the grave, and return to his waiting fellows.

I could picture Mendel turning pale, two streaks of sweat flowing down his cheeks. He might have had second thoughts, but honor wouldn't let him falter. I just knew he had been shaking as he took those old tefillin and headed for Shlomo's grave.

Nobody knows all that happened. Mendel did place the tefillin on the designated grave—they were found there the next morning.

Mendel, however, never left the cemetery, at least not by himself. His terrible shouts aroused the cemetery caretaker, who found Mendel upon the ground near the gates, screaming and thrashing about.

The story told in Szatmár was that as Mendel was approaching the grave closest to the exit, the last one he would need to pass on his way out, an image shrouded in a prayer shawl rose from behind the monument, spread its arms in a gesture of embrace, and moved toward Mendel.

Mendel never recovered his normalcy. His challenger, deeply

moved by the tragedy, became a recluse, spending all of his time in study, prayer, and meditation.

I still see Mendel as I saw him that evening after cheder. I have tried to envision how he might have looked just prior to the fateful moment when he made his decision to visit the dead. I deplore and bemoan the waste of this brilliant youth. He could have been a leader of his people.

When I arrived home, it was already ten o'clock, but fortunately for me my absence had gone unnoticed. There was a joyous occasion in progress in our neighborhood. Our Society of Charitable Piety was sponsoring the marriage of two poor orphans.

In later years I heard a different version of how Mendel went mad. As a scholar of mysticism, Mendel was deeply grieved by the prolonged suffering of Israel and the endless delay of the coming of the Messiah. Like many mystics before him, Mendel believed that it was in the power of even one individual, if properly prepared, to clear the road for the Redeemer.

Mendel decided to devote his entire life and all of his energies to the task of the redemption of Israel.

One day he took leave of his parents, telling them he would from now on spend all of his time at the synagogue. Secluded in one of the smaller rooms, he spent as many as twenty hours a day in study, contemplation, and reciting psalms. He concentrated on exercises of purification and penitence with the intent of summoning the prophet Elijah for an audience. Many before him, Mendel argued, had attained the privilege of revelation by Elijah. That achieved, Mendel would ask the prophet why Messiah was delaying his coming.

One night Mendel reached the climax of his penitential exercises. Remorsefully he chanted with the Yom Kippur melody: "O pour on us cleansing waters, as it is written, 'Then will I sprinkle clean waters upon you, and you shall be clean; from all your defilements will I cleanse you.' "

Hardly had Mendel finished his supplication when he heard a voice calling to him from the direction of the women's gallery. He looked up and saw a person with a white, long beard wrapped in a tallit.

"I have been sent to you from heaven; your prayers have been answered. Should I sprinkle you with cleansing waters?"

"Pour, O please, pour on me cleansing waters so that I may be clean," came Mendel's suppliant voice.

A bucketful of cold water then landed on Mendel's head, as a vicious laugh rent the silence and the awe of the night.

Early in the morning, the beadle opened the synagogue door and found Mendel unconscious on the floor.

Emanuel Grosinger, victim of the Holocaust.

Ilona Grosinger, victim of the Holocaust.

Imre Grosinger. "At the age of twelve he became an outcast, an undesirable, a non-person."

Author's father who perished at Auschwitz.

Author's paternal grandparents.

New high-rise complex at site of author's home, Satmar, 1984.

Satmar's Great Synagogue, 1984.

Burial site of soap made from the fat of Jewish victims, Satmar, 1984.

פ״נ
ספרי תורות
שנחדבו בעוהֺר בשנת"יִעֶברוֹם ועננו אֵותם
ונטמנו ביום חנוך בית הקברות החדש
ט׳ ימים לחדש טבת בשנת"ולחרלותנו „

Burial site of desecrated Torah-scrolls, Satmar, 1984.

16

The Prelude

THE PASSOVER SEASON of 1944 was sunny and warm. Some two weeks prior to the holiday I returned home to spend the festival with my parents and Shiele. I had been away for six months, studying at the yeshiva. During that semester, which turned out to be my last, I felt more homesick than ever before, and was looking forward with eager anticipation to the arrival of Passover. With Hershil and Yosil, my two older brothers, in hiding in Budapest in order to avoid conscription into one of the forced-labor brigades set up by the Hungarian government as part of its Nazi-influenced anti-Jewish program, I was now the oldest child at home.

On Wednesday, Szatmár's weekly market day, Shiele and I went to the marketplace to buy Passover essentials—potatoes, onions, eggs, horseradish, and a couple of chickens. Because of the new anti-Jewish laws that were now in force following the German invasion of Hungary, we went to the market after ten o'clock in the morning. The first hours of the day had been reserved, by law, for gentiles only, so that they could pick the choice produce and the best merchandise. Easily identifiable by the conspicuous yellow badge they were forced to wear, Jews had to be satisfied with whatever was still available after ten o'clock.

At home, mother meticulously scrubbed and cleansed our year-round cutlery, pots, and pans, readying them for the final step of ritual purification for Passover use. Families of limited financial means usually resorted to this method. They simply could not afford to maintain two full sets of kitchenware, one for everyday use and one for Passover, as required by Jewish law. Even so, we were always short of a cup, a dish, a glass, which had been taken out of the Passover set during the year to replace those broken by everyday use.

The replacement of these before Passover constituted an additional financial burden on our limited budget. Yet the joy and the sense of renewal that accompanied those activities more than compensated for the financial hardship.

A great fire was burning on the grounds of the Jewish community center. The guardian of the fire scrupulously fed its flames so that the highest possible temperature would be maintained. Above the soaring flames there was placed a huge kettle filled with boiling water, seething and foaming. From time to time, the attendant would pick a fiery-red brick out of the pyre and throw it into the boiling water. A wicker basket filled with cutlery would then be lowered into the boiling kettle, thus adding the final touch of Passover fitness to the silverware. Pots used for cooking required a similar process of purification, while pans used for roasting had to be heated red-hot on the flames.

Every year before Passover I liked to undertake this chore of the festival preparations. The conflagration, the seething waters, the red pyre all tremendously fascinated me. Inevitably, the vivid scene recalled to my mind the pyres of Molech, upon which little children had been burned as an offering to this wrathful god. Whenever I read in the Bible the repeated admonitions against this abominable practice, I was overtaken with deep remorse for the fate of those helpless children, whose cries had to be silenced with drumbeats.

My attention now turned to the beadle, who was in charge of the fire. I watched with fascination his dexterity in handling the flames, his method of pulling the fiery-red brick out of the pyre and lowering it into the hot water, his submerging of basketfuls of cutlery in the boiling kettle and then dipping them into cold water. Rather than a beadle, I looked at him as if he were a high priest officiating at a sacred service. His movements were swift, determined, and performed with deep concentration. To extract the hot brick from the fire, the beadle used two long tongs. He took special care not to splash hot water on the waiting public when lowering the brick into the seething kettle.

When my turn arrived, Reb Simchah—that was the beadle's name—motioned to me to put my cutlery and the pots into the basket. Now I could look at the water very closely, and I saw it boiling; just a few minutes earlier the beadle had dipped the hot stone in the kettle. Fully satisfied that the purification had been done properly, I returned home with a sense of deep relief. In the afternoon I returned to the center to pick up our matzot, the unleavened bread for Passover. Everything seemed ready now for the festival.

On the night before the Passover Eve, mother hid ten crumbs of bread at ten different spots in the house. Upon returning from synagogue, it was father's duty to search for, find, and remove those last vestiges of leaven from our domain. Both Shiele and I assisted father in the search. Normally, the ritual search for leaven was anticipated and conducted with eagerness and excitement. This time, however, there was no joy in our hearts. This was the first time that both Hershil and Yosil would be absent from the Seder festivities.

Besides, the wild rumors that had accompanied the German invasion of Hungary a few weeks earlier were in no way conducive to a festive mood.

Early in the morning of Passover Eve, I made a small fire in our backyard and burned the final vestiges of leaven accumulated in our search the previous night. It was the first time that father had entrusted me, now his oldest son at home, with the ritual burning of the leaven. As I watched the particles of bread consumed in the flames, I recited the traditional formula: "May all leaven in my possession, whether I have seen it or not, whether I have removed it or not, be regarded as nonexistent and considered as mere dust of the earth." Every nook and corner of our home was now permeated with the Passover spirit.

On the first night of Passover at synagogue there prevailed a festive, yet somber, atmosphere. The community of worshippers was composed of children, teenagers, and men over forty-five. All men betwen the ages of twenty and forty-five had already been conscripted into the notorious labor brigades, made up exclusively of Jews. Marked with yellow armbands, they were shipped to the Russian front to dig trenches and clear minefields for the Hungarian military and their German allies. Besides the high mortality they suffered as a result of mine explosions, they were often molested, maltreated, even shot to death, by their commanders.

When we returned home from the synagogue, mother greeted us with a smile and a warm welcome. The Seder table beckoned to us like a regal banquet, and soon we all found ourselves absorbed in the perennial tale of the exodus from Egypt. As if by a stroke of magic, all gloom and uncertainty disappeared. Elated by a spirit of hope and anticipation, we celebrated the Passover in a mood of great expectation. Drawing an analogy between the plagues inflicted on Pharaoh and the fragmentary news reaching us concerning German defeats on almost all fronts, we saw the end of tyranny close at hand. We did not know at that time that while our family and the rest of the Jews in Szatmár were celebrating the Passover with wine, hymns, matzot, and tasty food, the majority of European Jewry had already been gassed or starved to death. Nor did we suspect that our own days were numbered; that the door we had just opened for the prophet Elijah would soon be nailed and sealed behind us.

The German occupying forces had entered Szatmár toward the end of March. Rich in experience gained in other countries, special units of the SS moved ahead with ease and precision, mapping out plans for the Final Solution of Szatmár's Jewry. They did not have to act as strangers in a strange land. The Hungarian authorities eagerly cooperated with them. Nor was there even a ripple of protest forthcoming from any of the Hungarian churches.

Even before the German invasion, the Hungarian police made it a habit to stage raids in the streets and in homes with the purpose of rounding up "suspected Jews." The Jewish labor brigades had long been the scourge and the nightmare of every young Jewish man. No wonder everyone who could tried to evade this deathtrap. The method? Obtain a false identity which would make one younger, older, or gentile. It was obvious that one's looks had to conform with his newly claimed identity.

There was yet another group of Jews in Szatmár who had become the favorite target of police raids. A few dozen Polish Jews had succeeded in escaping Poland's slaughterhouses and making it all the way to Szatmár. These people had conveyed to us all they had witnessed in their own country, but no one would believe them. For anyone of either category to be caught by the police and his true identity exposed would have been tantamount to a death sentence.

My immediate older brother, Yosil, was three years my senior and subject to conscription for the labor brigades. He left home and went into hiding in Budapest, taking along with him a copy of my identity card. One Shabbat between Purim and Passover he came home to visit with father, mother, and his two younger brothers. On Shabbat morning, just as we were getting ready for synagogue, police raided our house. Terror befell us all. As the police searched the other apartments, mother began twisting her fingers in hysteria; father just turned pale, speechless. Yosil started pacing the room like a lunatic, looking for some opening in the wall or the floor where he could hide. There was no need for words. Should they find both of us, Yosil and me, with identical papers, the consequences would be dire. Yet there was nothing we could do.

Fortunately, salvation came at the spur of the moment, when it seemed that everything was lost. It came as a heavenly inspiration.

Our house had outdoor toilets, situated at the rear of the courtyard. While the police were checking the apartment of our immediate nextdoor neighbor, I slipped into the toilet and locked myself in. The toilet was close enough to our living quarters for me to hear the brutish insulting shouts of the police as they carried out their Jewhunt ritual.

"And what is your name?" one of them shouted loudly.

"Bernat Edelstein," came the answer in a steady, although slightly wavering, tone. It was my brother Yosil who had so identified himself, handing the policeman his papers for proof. All that time I was sitting in the toilet, heart pounding heavily, hands trembling nervously.

As soon as the identification ritual was over, father, Yosil, and Shiele left for synagogue. Then I heard one of the raiding party say to his colleagues that they ought to check the toilet to ascertain whether anyone was hiding there.

"Is there anyone inside there?" one of the raiding party shouted.

"Yes, I am here," I replied, but was in no hurry to open the door. My hunters became nervous and impatient, demanding loudly that the door immediately be opened.

I took my time, telling them that mother's chicken soup the previous evening was too fatty, and as a result I was now being plagued by diarrhea.

Slowly I pulled up my pants, buttoned my shirt and jacket, and fixed my hair. With Yosil by now out of reach and sight, I felt fully relaxed and confident, my previous nervousness completely dissipated. In fact, I started enjoying my new role. For a change, an entire squad of the Hungarian royal police had to wait in front of an outdoor toilet for a diarrhea-stricken Jewish boy to open the door for them.

Eventually, I opened the door.

"What is your name?" one of the party shouted.

"Bernat Edelstein," I calmly replied, handing him my identity card. He looked at the card, at me, then at his colleagues, and seemed somewhat puzzled. All the while, I stood there tensely awaiting his verdict. Somewhat embarrassed, he handed me the document without saying a word, then left with his company.

Hurriedly I walked into our home, where I found mother fighting back her tears. She embraced me and kissed me, and said nothing. There was no need for words. Without more delay I left for synagogue, but not the one where father and Yosil went to pray. Yet I saw to it that they received word of the good news of the happy ending.

Even while we were celebrating Passover, official surveyors were at work mapping out the future ghetto of Szatmár. A week or two later, "volunteer crews" were recruited among the Jews to erect the walls which would separate the Jewish population of Szatmár from its gentile population.

17

Into the Ghetto

HOW WELL I remember. The lilac tree at the rear of our courtyard stood in full bloom, but I was permitted to enjoy its loveliness only from a distance. I was forbidden to pick the flowers, forbidden even to stand near the tree more deeply to smell its fragrance. I looked at the tree and thought of Chanukah candles. They are sacred, can only be looked at, are not to be used for any practical purpose. Chanukah candles burn only to commemorate the victory in 165 B.C.E. of the Hasmonean priestly family over the Syrian-Greeks who sought to extinguish the light of Israel. Chanukah was months away, and yet there I stood by our door early that morning, thinking of the miracles and mighty deeds brought about by God on behalf of His people.

The truth is that the restriction against too fully enjoying spring flowers had arisen out of sorrow. Our lilacs bloomed sometime during the seven weeks between the festivals of Pesach and Shavuot. Once, these seven weeks had been the liveliest and most joyous days of the year. Following the ill-fated Jewish rebellion against the Romans in 135 C.E., the same weeks had been designated by the rabbis as a period of mourning in memory of those massacred in the defeat. Thus, nearly two thousand years later, I was forbidden our lilacs until the day of Shavuot Eve. Then we would decorate our home with flowers and shrubs in honor of the Torah, which was given to Israel on the festival of Shavuot.

In 1944 our Shavuot was preempted. Two weeks after Pesach, the walls of the Szatmár ghetto were completed, and the non-Jewish residents of the area encircled by the walls were moved out. The transfers completed, the herding got under way. Jews living in all parts of the city outside the walls were systematically sent into the ghetto. Our time had come. We received orders from the Hungarian authorities to be at home, to be ready to get out.

Days before, mother had finished making rucksacks. This she had done by hand, without a sewing machine, each stitch made in the midst of deep concentration. From time to time she had turned aside to wipe away a tear. Night after night I watched her sew in saintly devotion, seeing also those Israelite women of old who had spun goats' hair into yarn for the fabric of the Lord's tabernacle erected in the wilderness. Mother had made four sacks, one smaller than the others. The latter was for Shiele. Each sack had crisscrossing straps so that our loads might be eased. Even before our transfer day, we had trained ourselves in packing our rucksacks, filling them with essentials only, among which tefillin and Siddur had priority.

Most difficult for me was parting with my books. Carefully, and often at the cost of going hungry, I had during the years acquired a library of about thirty books. I could never have taken along all of them, so I tried to pick two or three favorites. I could come to no conclusion. Struggling not to cry, father had counseled me to leave all of them. He reasoned that there would be enough books in the many synagogues and Jewish homes encompassed by the ghetto. He further counseled me to make a list of my books and to take the list with me so that when eventually we returned home I could determine whether any books were missing.

I worried about my books and about Shiele. He admired me as his older brother and favorite storyteller. On the other hand, we had often quarreled and fought ferociously. One of our fights had ended with the blast of shattering glass. We had broken our door pane. Not until many days later could mother come up with the money for a new pane. But lately we hadn't fought. While things worsened and the ghetto walls were going up, a special bond of tenderness and love had developed between Shiele and me. More frequently than before, he sought my companionship. He had always been quiet and delicate, but now his paleness and his pensiveness were more obvious. Once he asked me to promise I would always be close to him, that I would never leave him. I promised, not knowing that forces stronger than I and more brutal than Satan would separate us forever.

Father in those days seemed detached, his heart and soul elsewhere. He would open a book, then soon close it. He hardly spoke at all. Yet again and again he said something about steadfastness and complete faith, always with a tremor in his voice. I saw him repeatedly open the drawer in which we kept over two hundred postcards written by his father, grandfather, and great-grandfather. The cards held both family history and Jewish wisdom. He would leaf through them, put them back into the drawer, take them out, and again replace them. I could sense that those cards meant a great deal to him.

I don't know how long I stood gazing at our lilacs, but it was Shabbat; we had a sacred duty to fulfill, and so I walked with father and Shiele to the synagogue. We left home earlier than was our custom, for we wanted to be back before the movers arrived. Never before had I experienced such strained worship. To begin with, the synagogue was half-empty; many friends who regularly prayed with us were not there. Still more disquieting, everyone present was highly nervous, seemingly anxious he would miss the opportunity to be taken into the ghetto. Indeed, though we were just where we should have been, we felt out of place. Our houses of study and worship, our homes and our shops, by decree, suddenly belonged to some power or another. Just as the dead must surely long to be taken to the cemetery, we felt a need to join our people already walled up in the ghetto.

By eight o'clock we were home again. Ordinarily, services would not have concluded before noon. During those hours, we youth had always managed to find a few minutes to relax, to talk about the confusions of the young, to create and strengthen friendships. Shabbat had always been for renewal, for rejoicing. At home, our Shabbat meal traditionally lasted for two hours or more. We would sing, exchange interpretations of Scripture, Mishnah, or Midrash. Sometimes, especially when we had guests at our table, our singing and discussion would continue until late afternoon. Afterwards, while our parents napped, we youngsters would socialize, play games, study.

This Saturday, this Shabbat was demolished. Mother nonetheless made a supreme effort to carry off some semblance of what used to be and should have been. Just as we had gone early to services, we now sat down early for our Shabbat meal. The traditional food and wine were on the table; we pronounced the blessings, but we did not sing. The meal was tragic, as sad as the one that preceded the fast of Tisha b'Av.

What was happening? For what good reason were we leaving our homes? Why were we Jews being separated and sealed off from the other citizens of Szatmár? What had we done wrong? When might we return to what was ours?

I was tormented to the point of exploding. The day was long, painfully long. Even by afternoon the movers had not arrived. We could only sit and wait. I began to wonder which of the four families living at 17 Batthany Street would be taken first. Would the movers start at the front of the building, or would they begin at the rear and take us first?

Our landlords, the Schroeders, a couple of about sixty-five, occupied the front lodgings. They never pressed for the rent when mother was late with it, as she often was. I do not remember their ever having been visited by children or grandchildren. The Schroeders liked to sit on their porch and always smiled at me when I passed by. If I helped them by running an errand to the market or by fetching a pail of drinking water from the city fountain, they would reward me generously. Both Shiele and I received frequent treats from them. The Schroeders were the only ones in our lodgings who did not follow strict Orthodox tradition. They originated from Germany; their dress was flawless, their manners refined. They were the antithesis of the stereotyped East European Orthodox Jew. Once, Mrs. Schroeder gently tried to convince me to conceal the fringes of my *tallit katan* under my shirt and to arrange my earlocks so that they would be less conspicuous. Such worldliness and drift toward heresy I could not abide, so I had fled from her as from temptation itself. Nonetheless, we had remained friends.

In the second lodging lived the Schwartz family. The father was a widower and an avowed follower of the Szatmárer Rebbe. He had two sons and three daughters. The younger son was about my age, seventeen. His adolescent sisters were a constant vexation for me. After all, my strict Orthodox upbringing strictly prohibited looking at a strange woman, and even at anything suggesting womanhood. Imagine then the discomfort created by the clothesline strung between two poles at the rear of the courtyard and readily visible from our window. Even when the girls were not in sight, their dresses danced in the breeze. Moreover, the youngest of the three sang most attractively when hanging wet laundry on the line. Alas, I had no sisters and had always wanted to ask my age-mate and neighbor just what it meant to dwell with such creatures.

The third lodging was taken by the Friedmans. They were quiet, just recently married. And of course, I wasn't supposed to look at her either, yet I knew she was pregnant. Her husband, who must have been nearly twenty-five, tried desperately to appear years younger. The results were often ridiculous, but then he was simply trying to avoid being blown to bits if sent off to the Russian front to clear minefields. While he waited for the authorities to catch up with him, he dealt in mushrooms. He would buy mushrooms wholesale and then bag them for distribution among the vegetable stalls of Szatmár. When the Friedmans couldn't handle all the bagging, I would help them in the evenings and turn my earnings over to mother. Sometimes only Mrs. Friedman and I would bag, while her husband secluded himself in another room to study Talmud.

But on this day, no one worked, no one studied. We waited, all of us—the Schroeders, the Schwartzes, the Friedmans, and the Edelsteins. Mrs. Schroeder was no longer concerned with my fringes and earlocks. For the first time, the presence of the Schwartz sisters did not distract me. Friedman did not conceal his age. None of these things mattered anymore. Neither did anyone attempt to hide or run. Only one determination served us all—to remain with family, come what may. In a world cold and hostile, future uncertain, there was only one warm spot left—one's own family.

Terrible things had been told by the Polish Jews who had come to hide in Szatmár. I didn't want to think about their stories and of the possible implications for me. Instead, I tried to fancy what life would be like when confined to a very small section of what used to be my city. I thought of my Shabbat afternoon walks in the park, situated at the very heart of Szatmár. In the summers, a military band would play there while large crowds, Jews and non-Jews alike, strolled about, enjoying both music and the cool breezes from the Szamos River. I thought of the many synagogues, chedarim, and yeshivot which the division of Szatmár had left outside the ghetto. I knew that soon, on a given day, at a given hour, all would be silenced. How would Szatmár look without its Jews? Would the gentiles be pleased to see us go? Would they feel remorse, shame?

I felt a slight touch upon my shoulder. It was Shiele, standing beside me, a faint smile on his face. I was glad to see him smile; he so seldom did. I wondered what he was thinking about, what doubts and fears tormented his young mind.

"Do you think, Beril, that Antshel, Marsha, and the baby are already in the ghetto?"

I was stunned. Thoughts about my oldest brother, his wife, and their two-year-old baby often invaded my mind, but they were too painful, and so I had always worked to dismiss them.

Nine years older than I, Antshel had been a strict disciplinarian. When I was younger, father had served as an itinerant rabbi, and was often away for days, sometimes a month at a time. Antshel was then head of the family; he had been especially difficult about my studies and my piety. He was the only one of the five sons who had not acquired a thorough talmudic education. He was the only of us to learn a trade; he had become a bookbinder. After he married, some three years earlier, he and his wife, Marsha, had moved to Nagyvárad, a two-hour train ride from Szatmár. While still a bachelor and living with us in Szatmár, my oldest brother practiced extreme piety. Although our own family was of limited financial means, he would often practice almsgiving with the last coins reserved for family essentials. Since Hershil and Yosil were at yeshiva, I was the one, while at home, who had to bear the brunt of his disciplinary measures. Yet I admired and respected his devotion to the advancement of my education and of my piety. Since the German invasion of Hungary we had received no message from Antshel, Marsha, and their baby. We knew that Marsha was now pregnant with her second child. My heart went out to them and to all the babies and the pregnant mothers. How would they manage this ordeal?

Even as Shiele was asking his question, we could hear the wagons rolling in the streets. The movers had arrived; I never answered Shiele.

The Hungarian police who were doing this phase of the Germans' dirty work were polite. The round-up system was by then well polished. We were told to reduce our belongings, our essentials. Where had we erred? Was it too much bedding, too many cooking utensils? Whatever it was, we left with rucksacks less full than we had planned.

I took a final look at my books, covered them with a sheet to protect them against dust, then stepped to the door. A last touch of fingertips upon our mezuzah, fingertips touched to lips, and I was out. Inadvertently I breathed deeply of our lilacs, wondered where we would this year pick flowers and shrubs for Shavuot.

The horses were given the order to move on. Father, mother, Shiele, and I followed the wagon as if in a funeral procession. The journey was short, only a few minutes, for we lived not far from the ghetto. The gate opened widely and closed immediately. We were now inside the ghetto. I felt a tremendous sense of relief; the ordeal was over, at least for the time being. I was again with my people. Thousands filled the streets, and there was a great commotion. I was dazed, not comprehending what was real and what a mirage.

18

Life in the Ghetto

OUR FAMILY OF four was allocated a room with a young couple and their only child of six years. For the sake of privacy we partitioned the small room with a blanket each night before retiring. The room adjacent to ours, and somewhat smaller, was occupied by a family of seven who had been brought to the ghetto from one of the smaller towns around Szatmár. There were no beds in the rooms; everyone had to sleep on the floor. Two members of the Fekete family were twin sisters, approximately my age. Both Dinah and Channah were vivacious, talkative, and great fun to be with. Mr. Fekete, from time to time, tried to restrain his daughters' airiness, but seemed to have lost control of them. The girls seemed to be enjoying the hustle and bustle of the ghetto, quite a contrast to the quiet and uneventful small-town life to which they were accustomed. Then again, perhaps they only affected a facade to conceal their real feelings of despair.

On my first night in the ghetto I came home late. Following services at synagogue I joined a group of people who were heatedly discussing the meaning of recent events. Diametrically opposing arguments were put forth by the various spokesmen, with equal convincing power. The optimists iterated the official line of the Jewish Council, echoing the German assertion that ghettoization was a temporary necessity due to the approaching front line. The pessimists, mainly Polish Jews, saw the worst coming. The listeners were inclined to agree with both sides, for the optimists represented wishful thinking, while the pessimists spoke from personal experience and presented sound arguments. The conversations brought no solace to my perplexities.

When I arrived at our room, that is, our part of the partitioned room, father, mother, and Shiele were already asleep. I saw that a spot had been reserved for me on the floor adjacent to the door separating our room from that occupied by the Fekete family. Quietly I lay down on the floor and covered myself with the blanket. The day just behind me had been fraught with overwhelming events, leaving me exhausted and shaken. I prepared for a good night's rest, though it would be on the floor; yet that was not how it turned out.

No sooner had I covered myself with blanket than I heard whispering voices. It did not take me too long to identify the voices as those of Dinah and Channah. It was then that I realized the girls were lying very close to me, just at the other side of the door. I could hear not only their conversation but also when they turned from one side to the other. The sisters had only one blanket to cover themselves with, for I heard them complaining to each other about pulling off too much blanket. I found myself in a predicament. Never before had I come so close to a girl even for a short time. Now I found myself lying close to two girls for the entire night. I could even hear their breathing. Besides, I thought it wrong not to let them know of my presence. I began to move about, to turn from one side to the other; I even coughed, yet all this came to naught. I wondered whether my messages weren't getting through. Had the girls decided to play a trick on me, or did they intend to entice me, a naive yeshiva student? Eventually, Dinah and Channah fell asleep. As for me, that night was destined to be a harrowing experience.

As I lay there on the floor in a strange place among strange people, robbed of every vestige of privacy, all the events of the past two or three weeks came to bear on me heavily. I could find no rest for my tired body, nor comfort for my wounded soul. I could not refrain from thinking of our home, humble as it was, from which we had been banished for no explicable reason. I wondered whether my books and the family collection of postcards were still where I had left them. Who was picking lilacs from our tree? The absolute lack of communication with my older brothers and the absence of any knowledge of their whereabouts and fate lowered my already depressed spirits. Father's and mother's pensiveness didn't help to cheer me up either. Under the circumstances, I felt a special responsibility for Shiele, who looked up to me for guidance and support.

Early in the morning all three families woke up simultaneously, as if by order. Partition removed, doors and windows opened, a flood of sunshine burst into the crowded quarters. I would have liked to stay a little longer in "bed," but circumstances prevented such luxury. Getting up, I felt more tired than I had been the evening before.

Recalling the previous night's events, I tried to avoid meeting Dinah and Channah. I felt somewhat guilty about violating their privacy. Still, I could only guess whether or not the girls were aware that I had been sleeping so close to them and listening to their movements and conversation. This ambiguity by itself caused me anxiety and confounded my line of action. Curiously, I now started paying closer attention to the sisters, trying to differentiate their resembling features.

As I was wont to do every morning since I could remember, on this my first morning in the ghetto I went to synagogue for the morning service. Strangely, the routine had hardly changed. Sure, the house of worship was more crowded than in normal times; services lasted somewhat longer, and there were many strangers in the synagogue. Yet in the structure of the service there was no change. Jews prayed as they had yesterday, the day before, centuries ago. No prayer was deleted, nor was a new one added. The present state of the Jewish people did not find expression in the format of prayer that morning, except for the sobbing that burst forth from many individuals. Life seemed to be returning to normal, the normalcy of the ghetto. There was no mass outcry against the great injustice, no outpouring demonstration against the monstrosities inflicted upon us. Jewish leadership had become paralyzed, disarmed of its vital signs.

Back at home, Dinah and Channah greeted me cheerfully, with warm smiles, and asked whether I had heard any news at synagogue. Deeply pleased with their manifestation of optimism and friendship, I engaged them in a conversation that considerably boosted my sagging spirits.

The second day in the ghetto was uneventful. More Jews were brought in, and we, the veterans, mobilized all of our skills and ingenuity to make life less painful and more tolerable. After all, we had no inkling as to how long we would be staying in the ghetto. Routine, even under abnormal circumstances, lends life a semblance of normality. On the surface, the ghetto resembled a vacation camp. Everyone was at leisure and didn't have to work. Children and adults alike were strolling the streets, talking politics and anything else their hearts desired. All social barriers had broken down, everyone having the same rights and privileges. Rich and poor rubbed shoulders. True, at the back of our minds lingered the frightful information we had heard from the Polish Jews; yet in our conscious minds we reasoned that the Russians would arrive before the Germans were able to do anything. Besides, the Germans who from time to time came to inspect the ghetto made a positive impression on us. They behaved in a civilized manner and spoke politely, much more politely than our own Hungarian police. It just did not make sense that they could be capable of doing the things they were rumored to have done.

The three families who shared the two adjacent rooms became ever more friendly and shared the daily chores. Much tact and patience were required to overcome the inevitable hardship and the taxing limitations, the most vexing of which was the inadequate toilet facilities. Most of the homes allocated for the ghetto were old and had poor sanitary systems. The influx of thousands more people exacerbated an already nearly intolerable situation. There was not as yet a serious shortage of food; most families had brought along provisions for at least one week, and the Jewish Council was providing for those in need. People who lived close to the wall were oftentimes surprised in the morning to find a few eggs on the ground, a bag of flour, a bottle of oil, and similar foodstuffs. Compassionate gentiles, under the cover of darkness, would slip those articles beneath the fence as a gesture of friendship or atonement.

When sleeping arrangements for the second night came up, I casually mentioned the possibility that I would sleep near the partition, rather than near the door; I did not elaborate. Both father and mother dismissed this option as impractical, advising me instead to sleep adjacent to the door, where I had slept the previous night. They obviously thought it inappropriate for me to sleep close to a partition of a mere blanket on the other side of which there was a young couple sleeping. Indeed, who could say which alternative was to be preferred?

On the second night, Dinah and Channah had separate blankets with which to cover themselves. At least that was my conclusion, for I did not hear them quarrel over this issue any more. In fact, I did not hear them speak at all. I hoped my presence was by now known to them, and that was the reason for their silence. I was wrong. Before long, the silence was broken, and I heard sobbing mingled with words that I could not decipher. Nor could I determine which of the two sisters was sobbing and uttering words intermittently. I listened, flabbergasted, not knowing what to do. Then I heard a voice, clear and articulated, yet compassionate and caressing. It was Dinah's voice.

"Have you finished your prayer?"

There was no answer. A tense moment of silence followed.

"Do you really believe prayer would make any difference?"

"If I did not believe so, I would not be praying."

"Well, often we do things and say words out of sheer habit, without really contemplating what we are saying or doing."

"I don't understand you. What do you mean?"

"What I mean is that all of our prayers are full of yearnings to go up to Zion and Jerusalem. Yet have we ever done anything to make those prayers a reality?"

"What could we have done except pray?"

"I remember, about two years ago, a Zionist agent came to our town and spoke at the synagogue about a possibility that existed for some to emigrate to Eretz Yisrael, to Palestine. He had a beard, earlocks, and looked just like one of our Jews. It was the first time I had seen a Jew who came from Palestine. Yet our Rabbi had him expelled. He even threatened excommunication for anyone who entertained such a heretical idea as going to Palestine. Had we listened to that Jew, instead of just praying, we wouldn't be here now in this accursed place, expecting the worst."

"Yes, I remember him. I remember his flaming eyes, his pointed red beard dancing up and down as he spoke of great opportunities beckoning to us before the eleventh hour, before it would be too late. He spoke of the flourishing villages and farms our people had built in the land of Israel. He spoke of the new Jew—free, unafraid, and uninhibited—who was growing up in our ancestral land."

"Yet our rabbi had him expelled! Why?"

"Our rabbi believes that Jews ought to pray and wait for the coming of the Messiah, who will, in God's own good time, take us all to the land of Israel. Until such a day comes, our rabbi says, we can only pray and hope. It is sinful, the rabbi says, to try forcing God's timetable. Besides, the rabbi says that many Jews who live in the land of Israel have discarded our sacred traditions and have become a people like all the nations."

"Well, what is wrong with becoming like all the nations? Do you take great pride in being singled out and marked by this yellow rag for ridicule and abuse? Do you enjoy lying here on this floor, herded together like chickens in a coop?"

"I still believe that prayer may avert the worst. Don't you?"

"No, I don't. That's why I didn't pray tonight."

"When did you stop saying your night prayers?"

"The very day we were herded into our synagogue to be taken from there to this accursed place. All that night, my first night ever away from home, I was looking at the eternal light, which was suspended directly over me. I had always believed the eternal light represented God's eye watching over His people. That night, witnessing the shame and humiliation His faithful had to endure in His very house, I began asking myself whether He really sees or cares."

"You should not be uttering such words, Dinah. What you are saying is sheer blasphemy. Perhaps our rabbi was right, after all. Those who are attracted to Zionism, the rabbi said, eventually drift away from our sacred traditions."

For a moment it seemed as if the twins had exhausted their arguments and that this extraordinary conversation had reached its conclusion with Channah having the final say. I felt both relieved and agonized. For one thing, I felt quite uncomfortable in the role of a passive and invisible partner. On the other hand, I was fascinated with the conversation and would have liked it to continue. I didn't have to wait for too long before Dinah made her final reply.

"It was not Zionism, but our elders' blind opposition to it, that made me say the words I have just said. Uncle Borech, who ignored the rabbi's opposition to Palestine, now sleeps in Haifa in his own bed, in his own home."

I was about to explode. I had always thought of girls as having circumscribed interests and limited information. After all, they did not attend yeshiva, nor could they listen to the discussions of the wise at the synagogue. Yet here I had just witnessed a profound exposition of the most cardinal issue on the Jewish agenda. All this from two girls my age!

I envied Dinah and Channah. I too had searing doubts and gnawing questions, but there was no one with whom to discuss them openly. Shiele was too young and too pensive. Father wouldn't be inclined to discuss such a hot issue; he would never admit the slightest doubt in a matter of faith. Unflinching faith was his personal guideline, and faith he counseled to others, too. How I wished I could join in the conversation with Channah and Dinah. Their very candidness in honestly tackling the issue came as a refreshing breeze. But if I joined, I would have betrayed my listening, uninvited, to their conversation. Besides, a tripartite conversation with a door in between would almost certainly have awakened all three families; that was the last thing I wanted to do that night.

Silence, thick silence, descended upon our crowded dwelling place. Then, the sudden cry of an infant pierced the stillness of the night. More babies joined, and young mothers tried pacifying them. From the street just opposite my window, the pacing steps of two guards disturbed the solemnity of the night. From the other side of the door I again heard sobbing. This time, unmistakably, there were two distinct voices sobbing simultaneously, Dinah and Channah, embracing and kissing, trying to confort each other. My heart went out to them. Again the pacing guards marched past my window. One of them now said something in a voice that betrayed his drunkenness, and both burst into wild, ugly laughter. I felt a deep aversion to this wanton defilement of the holiness of the night. Then there was silence again. Everyone seemed to be asleep. Everyone but me.

On the morning of the third day, the three families woke up even earlier than the day before. Father was always first to get up. After he had poured water on his fingertips to remove the night's impurities from them, he passed the bowl of water and the basin to mother, to me, and to Shiele. Impurities thus removed, I was now ready to utter the first words of prayer while still in bed.

> I render thanks to Thee, everlasting King, who hast mercifully restored my soul within me; Thy faithfulness is great. The Torah which Moses handed down to us is the heritage of the house of Jacob. May blessings rest on my head. Hear, my son, your father's instruction, and reject not your mother's teaching. The Torah shall be my trust, the Almighty my help.

This short morning prayer was taught to children at a very early age. They knew it by heart even before they learned to read. I had repeated those words thousands of times with eyes still half-closed. These words were instrumental in inculcating a purpose and a meaning into life. One did not get up in the morning into a void, purposeless. Time is imbued with sacred dimensions. To squander even a fragment of it was considered the height of folly. As the child grew older, many similar admonitions were brought to bear on his impressionable mind, such as the maxim of Judah ben Tema: "Be bold as a leopard, light as an eagle, fleet as a hart, and strong as a lion, to do the will of thy Father who is in heaven."

That morning, however, left me wondering about the purpose of our being in the ghetto. I had neither the boldness of a leopard nor the lightness of an eagle. I awoke more tired than I was when I went to bed. What would the coming night be like, and the night after? How many more nights, weeks, perhaps months, would we be forced to spend in this chicken coop? What would be the next stage?

A pleasant sound interrupted my thoughts. Dinah had entered our room with a broad smile on her ruddy face and with a resounding "Good morning." She had come to ask for some household item from mother. Her pinkish cheeks made a perfect blend with the two raven-black braids of hair dangling down her shoulders. Soon, Channah followed her with some other excuse. Neither of the sisters seemed to be in a hurry; they stayed in our room and engaged mother in conversation. As I was now watching the two sisters very closely, I noticed that Dinah's hair was of a deeper hue than Channah's. Like her sister, Channah had her hair arranged in two long braids gliding down her shoulders. Both girls had their braids gracefully adorned with red ribbons.

Instinctively I touched my two earlocks and was satisfied they were perfect. Yet, noticing the small mirror hanging on the wall, I moved over to it as inconspicuously as possible and observed my earlocks again.

"Your earlocks, Beril, are perfect. You, certainly, know how to curl them."

I startled and blushed. Without even having to look, I identified the voice as that of Dinah. There was warmth and sincerity in it. As I turned toward her to acknowledge the compliment, I saw Channah smiling and nodding approvingly. I felt both elated and embarrassed. It was the first time I had ever received a compliment from a girl.

The evening service was over; the synagogue was unusually crowded. There was a hush among the worshippers, and an air of expectation. The rabbi was yet to pronounce the blessing and the counting of the Omer. Ordinarily, the daily counting of the Omer during the seven weeks between Pesach and Shavuot would not take up more than a few minutes. These, however, were no ordinary times; the fate of Israel was hanging in the balance. Every individual, in accordance with his merits and ability, was called upon to exert himself to the utmost in tipping the scales favorably.

Although the counting of the Omer recalls a harvest rite of Temple days, the sages of the Kabbalah invested this ritual with mystical meaning. In their view, the omnipresence of the Almighty is effectuated through His ten spheres, or emanations, the first of which is designated as "Crown," and the tenth as "Kingdom." Of the ten spheres, the last seven and their various combinations represent the seven weeks, or the forty-nine days of the Omer. These seven emanations, if properly combined and pronounced in a mood of sacred concentration, may have a profound impact on the conduct of the world, even on the state of its salvation.

On that particular evening, the rabbi was in a trance. Pacing the synagogue between two rows of worshippers—eyes closed, face red, and emitting streams of sweat—he was reciting psalmodic utterances incoherently. At times he would stop and freeze on the spot, then resume pacing. A half-hour passed, and the worshippers still waited, spellbound, for the rabbi to pronounce the blessing and the day's counting. Tension ran high. Why was the rabbi prolonging this otherwise short ritual? What was he up to?

Then palefaced, as though awakening from a dream, the rabbi began addressing the public, his voice trembling, his body shaking.

"Why has all this come upon us, you ask. Why has God afflicted us so much? I will tell you why. God is punishing us for our arrogance, our vainglory, and our rebelliousness. Have we put our trust in our Father who is in heaven? No. We have brazenly tried to rely on our wisdom instead of pleading for mercy to the Almighty. We have tried to force the hands of God with untimely solutions, solutions that hold no cure to our troubles, solutions that are mere vanity. They have tried to force upon us a godless Zionism, denying or forgetting the messianic hopes which alone can sustain us in our dispersion, and which alone are the source of our salvation. 'Unless the Lord builds a house, its builders toil in vain,'" the rabbi's voice thundered above the heads of the flabbergasted worshippers.

He spoke for about half an hour, reiterating and belaboring the same theme again and again. The poor worshippers, hard crushed beneath the heel of the oppressor, physically and mentally exhausted, disciplined and trained for generations in self-flagellation, responded with sobbings and sighs. It was a long time before everyone quieted down and the rabbi could resume again, this time with a tone of hope and promise. When finished, he turned toward the holy ark, pronounced the blessing, and cried out, "Today is the thirty-third day, being four weeks and five days in the counting of the Omer." Following the recitation of a few more verses, he pronounced the mystic combination of the day as "Supreme Majesty." The service came to an end, and the worshippers left for their homes, strengthened in their faith.

Observant Jews do not cut their hair and do not marry during the days when the Omer is being counted, for the same reason that they do not pick or smell lilacs. However, the thirty-third day, known as Lag ba'Omer is an exception.

Speaking esoterically of the tragic results of the Bar-Kokhba uprising, the rabbis related the following episode: "Rabbi Akiva had twenty-four thousand disciples, all of whom died in his lifetime between Pesach and Shavuot because they did not show respect for each other. As a result, the world became desolate." Tradition has it, however, that on the thirty-third day they ceased dying; therefore, it was proclaimed a semiholiday, and activities prohibited on the other days of the Omer were now permitted.

Thus, in the morning, the ghetto began to resemble a huge barbershop. Wherever I turned I saw people having haircuts. In normal years Lag ba'Omer was also the occasion of many weddings. This year, however, most of the marriageable men had been carried away to the Ukrainian battlefields, where many had already been killed. Those in the ghetto were in no mood to get married. Haircutting, however, was a booming business.

Although no major holiday, Lag ba'Omer did bring a respite in the midst of a prolonged mourning period; even children benefited from it. In cheder days, our rabbi would permit us to go to the nearby woods where we made bows and arrows and aimed them at the trees. One day a year, even though only for a short hour, I experienced a meaningful metamorphosis. I became a soldier. There in the thick of the forest I ferociously fought all the enemies of Israel. Amalek, I blinded his right eye; no more would he send marauding bands to cut off the stragglers in the rear of Israel's tired masses. Sihon and Og, the two giant kings, I could aim only at their knees. My most piercing arrows, however, I saved for Titus, who burned the Temple and carried our people away into exile. Nor did I forget my real enemies, the boys my age and older who used to attack me at school and in the street, pulling my earlocks and taunting me because—so they said—I had killed the Savior.

How far away were those days! How remote that forest! Now, here in the ghetto, there were no arrows or archers, but the enemy was very real.

As I walked through the streets of the ghetto, watching the many haircuts being given, my attention was especially drawn to the three-year-olds who were having their first haircuts. I remembered how I used to clip the hair of the little ones at the mikveh court on Fridays. I remembered how timid and submissive they were. Now I was watching them from a different angle, that of a bystander. Some trembled, others cried, yet all knew what was expected of them.

In normal years, it was the father who took the three-year-old to the barber for his first haircut. Now I saw many mothers accompanying their little ones to the barbar, for their husbands had been taken away to the labor brigades. My own uncle Fishel had been drafted into the brigades on the very day he had performed the circumcision of his fifth child. His wife Judith and their five children were then taken to the ghetto. When my uncle returned after the war, he found neither his wife nor any of their children.

Life in the ghetto began to assume a pattern of normalcy. It has been noted that a cat and a Jew, wherever you throw them, always land on their feet. Had the Germans only left us alone, we might have waited out the war, but the Germans had other plans for us. They had not come all this distance only to herd us into a ghetto.

Early one morning when everyone was still sleeping, German trucks drove into the ghetto and into our street. In a few minutes, everyone was rounded up, ordered into the trucks and driven to the small ghetto. Body searches were conducted again and valuables confiscated. The people who had lived in the small ghetto had already been deported before our arrival. Now we knew it was only a matter of days until we too would share the same fate. There was not even a semblance of hope. Instead of longing for our homes outside the ghetto, we now yearned for the ghetto of yesterday. Everything seemed lost, hopeless.

In the little ghetto there was no longer any organized communal life. Everyone was left to himself and had to care for himself. No one even tried putting some order into chaos. There was only one question on everyone's mind. When would they come, today, tomorrow, or the day after? Then there was another, though unspeakable question. Where will they take us?

This time there was no horse and wagon; everyone had to carry his bundle by himself. In that humble rucksack lay the last remnants of the hard work and diligent enterprise of many generations. Mothers of young children had to carry, in addition, their children. There was no pity, no mercy.

It had been a breezy afternoon, followed by a cool evening. We started our march along Toltés Street, which runs parallel to the Szamos River. I helped father, mother, and Shiele lift their rucksacks and adjust them on their backs. Shiele thanked me with a faint smile. Father's face was aflame like the setting sun. He avoided looking at my eyes. He had no words of comfort. Mother was expressionless and speechless. The streets we passed through were deserted; as we marched along, there was no one else to be seen. From some porches and windows people gazed at us in bewilderment; a few waved their hands, none spoke a word. The procession moved listlessly, monotonously; only infants' cries broke the thickness of the silence. I looked at the familiar places where I used to stroll with friends and wondered when I would see them again.

At the railway station there was a long line of boxcars, attended by armed gendarmes. There was no trouble, no resistance. With typical obedience, everyone climbed orderly into the designated boxcar, while the gendarmes counted. When the desired number was reached, counting for the next car began. Each car, when filled to its utmost capacity, was shut tight with a loud bang. Then came the long wait for departure. The Germans saw to it that there was always an expectation for something, although unknown, that might be an improvement on the present situation.

Except for an episode related in another chapter of this book, I do not recall anything of the three-day journey from Szatmár to Auschwitz. It has been entirely blocked from my memory. In discussions with other survivors, I have found this to be true with many of them. I do not remember whether I talked about anything at all with my parents or with Shiele during those most fateful days in our lives. I don't remember what we did during those three days. In fact, I don't remember any of the people who were with us in the boxcar. Many times I have tried to focus concentrated attention on that journey in an effort to recapture some of the sights and events, or some of the words that were spoken, but always to no avail. Almost everyone, however, vividly remembers the first impact of Auschwitz following detrainment. Mountains of suitcases and rucksacks, and ascending flames that redden the skies over a large area is something one does not easily forget.

Father always wore a large-sized *tallit-katan*, its four fringes conspicuously visible, in fulfillment of the biblical injunction, "that ye may look upon it and remember all the commandments of the Lord, and do them; that ye go not astray after the desires of your heart and of your eyes." Hardly had we disembarked from the train when a furious SS guard approached father and tore off one of his fringes, throwing it away in disdain as though it were a defilement. This queer incident had a disquieting effect on me. In Jewish tradition, a dead man is to be buried in his prayer shawl, but not before one of its four fringes has been torn away and separately placed in the coffin. Yet there was no time to contemplate the possible significance of this incident, for the line had to move on to the selection station, and from there to the showers.

Before entering the showers, I was stripped naked and my hair was shorn. When I saw my two earlocks drop to the ground, I instinctively bent down to pick them up. I was clubbed on both of my hands by one of the guards. The loss of my earlocks affected me as if two of my fingers had been cut off. For weeks, perhaps months, even in my sleep, I would often touch the spots on my skull where once I had two beautiful earlocks. I felt two gaping wounds.

Showers taken, everyone was given a striped garment, the uniform of the prisoner. At first, we did not recognize each other. Then, some burst into sobbing cries, while others laughed hysterically. For the night we were locked into a huge empty barracks. There was neither toilet nor water. We spent the first night in Auschwitz sitting or lying on the wet, muddy floor.

Not being able to fall asleep, I wondered about father, mother, and Shiele. Why had we been separated? Whereto had they been taken? Would we be reunited tomorrow or sometime later? Why had we been brought to this strange destination in the first place? What was going to happen to us here?

It was only later that I found out what happened to Dinah and Channah, the two beautiful, kind twin sisters. They were last seen when taken to the barracks where "medical" experiments were being conducted on Jewish twins under the personal supervision of Dr. Mengele. They were never seen again, nor heard of.

19

Phylacteries

On the third day, as morning dawned, there was thunder, and lightning, and a dense cloud upon the mountain, and a very loud blast of the
horn; and all the people who were in the camp trembled. . . . Now
Mount Sinai was all in smoke, for the Lord had come down upon it in
fire; the smoke rose like the smoke of a kiln, and the whole mountain
trembled violently.

—Exodus 19

OUR TRANSPORT FROM Szatmár arrived in Auschwitz on the
third day of our journey at sunset. It was the eve of the festival of
Shavuot (Pentecost). Like my ancestors assembled around Mount
Sinai three millennia earlier, I too saw smoke and flames rising like
steam from a kiln. There were screams and shouts that made all of us
tremble.

Of all of the personal belongings that I had left behind in the train,
the loss of my phylacteries weighed most heavily on my mind. True,
I would not need them for the two days of Shavuot, as tefillin are not
worn on the Sabbath or on festivals. But what about the day after
Shavuot? I simply could not conceive of not putting on tefillin even
for one day. Would our belongings be returned to us during the next
two days?

As I was so preoccupied with my tefillin on my first day in
Auschwitz, I remembered the day I first donned them on my forehead and on my forearm. It was a Monday, my Bar Mitzvah day.

My second year at yeshiva, the rebbe placed the hand phylactery
on my left biceps muscle. Then he proceeded to coil its black leather
strap around my arm seven times. The strap pressed tightly against
my flesh. When the morning service was over and I removed the

86

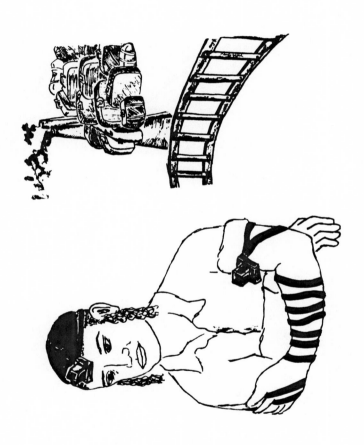

tefillin, I noticed the deep traces the tight strap had left in my soft flesh, still another sign of the Covenant. Seeing this new sign in the flesh on my Bar Mitzvah day, I felt elated. Father, who attended the event, was overjoyed.

Now that I had been stripped of my tefillin, a story I had heard several years before vividly impressed itself on my mind.

A widow once came to the rebbe and told him that in a dream she had seen her freshly buried husband lying in his coffin, a snake coiled around his left forearm, and two frogs well entrenched, one on his forehead, and one on his left arm. When the dream kept recurring, each time with more violent consequences to her mental health, the rebbe ordered the grave opened so that the woman would be convinced it was only a dream. To everyone's astonishment, however, the dead body was found exactly as described by his wife's dreams. A short investigation by the rebbe revealed that the man, while alive, was negligent in the performance of the mitzvah of tefillin.

I shuddered.

To sneak a watch or a ring into Auschwitz was out of the question. To bring in even a pin was an impossibility. If one had succeeded in concealing something prior to being herded into the ghetto, he more than likely gave it up when leaving for the railroad station. Even he who for days had ignored the threat of being shot if found in possession of valuables finally gave up his treasure upon reaching the camp. There everyone was stripped naked.

How then had a pair of phylacteries made its way into Buna, the subdivision of Auschwitz to which I was assigned? That remained a mystery, perhaps a miracle. Yet there they were nonetheless.

The most dreaded moment in the camp was wake-up. Shrill whistles and pagan shouts tore my solitude to shreds. All night long I had been free of their tormenting presence, had woven dreams. My future was ever the same: a whole loaf of bread. I held it oven-hot and throbbing in my brick-torn hands. Not an eighth, nor a quarter, not even a half, but an entire loaf of bread, mine, all mine.

At times, finally satisfied with bread eaten at leisure, I would help myself to a full bowl of steaming soup, dense with potatoes and cereal. Yet hardly had I touched my soup before the sirens slammed into my chest. *Aufstehen! Aufstehen!* Wake up! I was again a *Häftling*, a prisoner.

No sooner out of the bunk than I was in line for my shower. Our bodies were shrinking but free from filth. For as slave laborers we were useful cogs in the machinery of the German industrial plants set up in the Auschwitz area, and who among the executives heading these enterprises would have wished our souls spirited away by an epidemic before our limbs had worked their last?

Both summer and winter the showers were ice cold. Wet and shivering, I was shoved to the coffee line, ersatz coffee, a quarter-loaf of bread, a taste of margarine or sausage. Then another push and, still gulping my rations, I was shoved toward where we were counted before marching to the gates and to work.

Shower lines and coffee lines. A line at the latrine, and a line for a haircut or to replace a broken shoe, if you were lucky. For everything a line.

And yet there was one more line when time and chance permitted. A line that belonged exclusively to some of us who had not forsaken God, even though at times it seemed as if He had forsaken us. It was a line that had not been ordered by our tormentors. They were even not aware of its existence.

Those of us who dared came hurriedly to the end of the barracks, to a line between two rows of bunks. There we stole a moment to touch, hold, and kiss our single pair of smuggled phylacteries. Blessing pronounced, the phylacteries would swiftly be touched to forearm and forehead, then surrendered to the next in line.

Often not enough time was available for all waiting to receive the phylacteries. Those who were forced to leave disappointed would come to the line even earlier the next morning.

Then it happened. Our kapo's assistant chanced upon our line. For a second or so he stood motionless and expressionless, watching as the phylacteries quickly changed hands.

He was not more than fifteen or sixteen years old. He was the rare adolescent survivor, one who lived by being errand boy, spy, and yes, lover, for a block supervisor or for a kapo. That boy had life, and he had power.

The phylacteries were now in the hands of a Jew of about forty. I was third behind him. Suddenly, as this man was about to bring the phylactery to his lips, the boy fell into a rage. Shouting, he began to hit the man with his billy.

"Who are you praying to, you old goat? How can you be such a fool to pray to a God who has done this to you?"

Turning to all of us, he screamed, "You will not get out of here alive! You, all of you, will turn into smoke and ashes!"

He then took the phylacteries, threw them to the ground, and trampled upon them, cursing all the while. One of the group endeavored to save the holy objects from further desecration. The boy struck at him without mercy until the phylacteries dropped once more upon the floor.

There was never again a sacred line in our barracks. Agewise, the man beaten could have been the father of the young boy. Was that youth ever a Bar Mitzvah? Had he once had phylacteries of his own? Did those blows fall not upon the stranger but upon a father for having abandoned a son experiencing loss of self, destruction of soul?

And whom should the world fear and pity more, he who destroys, or he who suffers destruction?

20

The Knife

FOR A RAW potato you could have a cigarette. Exchange enough of your starvation fare and you could make selection sooner than most, your emaciated body sliding up the chimney in a pillar of smoke.

I didn't want a cigarette, not even a sweater; my business at the black market was a small sharp knife. Price, half a loaf, two days' ration of bread. Repeatedly, I dreamed of having a knife but could never risk that much food. Then one evening I was offered such terms that I couldn't withstand the temptation. For the cost of a knife, I was offered both a knife and a spoon. Even better, I could pay the half-loaf in four consecutive days, one-eighth of a loaf per day, leaving an equal portion for myself. A deal was struck.

Knife in hand, I was happy. I cut my bread into small squares, slowly chewed each bit, wandered for hours in the wilderness of Sin, listening for quail, expecting dew by morning.

After evening rations, we talked about the day's events, speculated about tomorrow. Nobody ever mentioned, not even in one word, what had been before we came to this place. The subject was too frightening to touch.

We talked a bit, then each prisoner retreated to his bunk, there to be fully with himself, his loneliness, his agonies, his searing doubts.

Eyes shut tight, fists clenched, once more a fetus curled within my mother's womb. I was borne each night to things that once had been. An image, a sound, fragrances, names; fragments of a world ripped asunder surged and ebbed in the darkness. I prayed for light, for hope, for meaning. I implored the Almighty, praised be He, that the flow of fragments would never cease.

I prayed.

Something was violating my face, its touch coarse and ugly. I thought to remove it, found my hands incapable of response. I tried to believe that what was happening to my face was actually happening to the one on the bunk below, that I shouldn't concern myself with something happening to someone else. The gnawing did not subside; it quickened, tensing my nerves to the limit. In concentrated effort, I summoned both my hands and, with a force I didn't imagine my hungry limbs possessed, I struck the spot of agony. Blood covered my face, a hideous rot invaded my nostrils, forcing me almost senseless.

I had killed a bedbug.

Bedbugs became the scourge of my nights. No sooner did I fall asleep than the merry-go-round procession started. Sleep became almost impossible.

21

The Potato

LIFE RAPIDLY BECAME routine, the abhorrent, familiar, though no less terrifying.

I had the third, the uppermost bunk. From there, I could watch the soup line inching toward our most substantial meal. Since the one distributing the soup never bothered to stir the kettle, all the vegetables and cereal would sink to the bottom. I soon learned to estimate how many servings would bring an additional measure of life within my grasp, learned when I should join the line so that my turn would find me before the kettle just as the dense part of the soup had been reached. Often, my calculations worked. When they failed, I waited, bowl in hand, just as the kettle was being changed. Then I ate, drank something which only an idiot would consider soup.

Like all the other prisoners, I lost much weight, became exhausted and listless. My fellows looked at me, doubted my chances.

Then one afternoon upon our return from forced labor, the block supervisor barked out ten numbers. One, two, three, four . . . A-7868. I had been chosen, not for selection, but for a transfer.

I loved within an instant my new block, my new bunk. At last I could escape the bedbugs which made sleep all but impossible. I could dream of the young David, recall the Midrash wherein David asked the Lord God why He had created the spider and was told, "Wait, and you will see." I could flee, follow David into the cave, sit there beside him as despondent King Saul stormed the site, but when seeing the intricate web covering the entrance, bid his officers leave and search elsewhere. I am still wondering, though, for what good purpose God created the bedbug.

I could sleep, I could dream.

Lying early one evening in bed, I felt a slight irritation in my left leg. I looked at it and saw a red spot, no bigger than a pinhead. I ignored it. In the morning, the redness had spread to a larger area, and there was also swelling. By the third day I had started to limp; hobbled out to join my work unit.

As we marched past the band formed of musician inmates, special SS guards watched our feet. A single misstep might mean a new pair of shoes or a beating, who could tell?

I made a supreme effort to keep in step; I couldn't. Pointing with his officer's baton, a guard motioned for me to fall out and approach him. I showed him my swollen leg and received a written order to report immediately to the infirmary.

Never before had I seen the camp as it appeared on that morning. I had known only massed thousands, only lines for soup, for coffee, to exchange torn pants, to get a haircut, to be counted, to enter a shower.

The air seemed thinner, brighter, smelled fresher than ever before. For the first time I had ample room to move about. No shoving, no pushing; just calm, peacefulness. Emptied of the bulk of its slaves, Buna appeared larger, the sun softly caressing. Even the guards in the watchtowers smiled at me from above their machine guns.

My leg stopped bothering me. I strolled through the camp, my nose finally pulling me toward the kitchen. I stopped a short distance away. Before me stood huge boxes filled with bread; around me towered mounds of potatoes, carrots, onions, the aromas cutting, unbearable.

It really wouldn't make any difference, would it? Even if I ate all day, it wouldn't show, it wouldn't make any difference, except for me. Who really would mind if I just went ahead and started helping myself? How should I know?

Never had I encountered such an overwhelmingly strange situation.

How long did I stand there?

How many millennia before my hand began reaching for the potato which had, prior to my arrival, separated itself from the pile and now lay, like manna from heaven, just before my feet?

A pain shot through my arm, a scream tore from the back of my throat, I turned, came face-to-face with an SS man who had been tracking my movements.

He demanded an accounting. I showed my infirmary directive. Again, I felt the force of his rubber billy, applied with orders to run, run to the infirmary.

When I got there, I didn't know whether to show the doctor my flaming buttocks, my bruised and aching arm, or my throbbing leg.

22

The Infirmary

DR. DREYFUS SPOKE with me in Yiddish. Following a brief examination, he diagnosed my trouble as phlegmon, an inflammation of the subcutaneous tissue, saying he would operate the next day.

Never before had I been hospitalized. Although assured that the procedures were but minor surgery, I was frightened. Would my leg heal? Would I be able to work again?

Looking around, I noted that the other patients ranged in age from thirty-five to forty-five. I was the youngest, eighteen.

Some of the sick were skeletal, their bones obvious in a manner both pitiful and horrifying. I had heard of, but had not previously seen, these Muselmen, the living dead.

Was I going to become one of them? Would I too ultimately be carried off to some convalescent home? Where? I could not contain the questions erupting from the depths of my being.

Where were my mother, my father, my younger brother Shiele, all those who came with me?

The orderly showed me my bed, white sheets and a soft blanket. A window beside my bed was curtained. Here and there were potted plants. Music flowed from the physicians' quarters, sunlight flooded the sickbay. For a moment, I forgot realities.

These curtains, who had hung them in the hospital? Were they from Holland? from Belgium? The child who once played beneath these flowered curtains, how old had she been? Had her mother sewn them, purchased them in Amsterdam or Brussels? For a birthday, just for love? Where was that little girl, and where was her mother?

And the piano, did it come from some other quarter, Hungary perhaps? The painting on the western wall in the chief physician's room, from whose home had that been taken?

My own collection of some two hundred postcards, written by my

94

grandfather and by my great-grandfather, and covering a family history of more than sixty years, where were they? Our most precious heirloom, they were safeguarded by my father, the oldest of eleven children. Though they were kept in a locked drawer, I often secretly went to them, fascinated by the stamps, but more so by the tiny Hebrew in which they were written. I read those dense lines, learning of aunts and uncles whom I had never met.

Ordered out of our home, we were permitted only a small bag of essentials. All else, we were told, would be held in safekeeping until we returned at the war's end.

Might those cards yet remain in that locked drawer? Was the cabinet with the drawers still in our home?

I felt a hand caressing my forehead. Opening my eyes, I recognized Dr. Dreyfus. Taking my hand and looking into my eyes, he smiled, yet that smile could not change the sorrow glazing his own eyes.

Later, he would tell me about his son, seventeen when they had arrived here two years before. He would speak of his wife and daughters, also last seen at the gates.

They had lived thirty-five miles from Paris, the family having settled there four generations before and having developed extensive vineyards.

The doctor recalled the enormous vats containing thousands of liters of wine. As a small child, he never understood how those vats belonging to his grandfather could be emptied. Even if the whole town and all the people round about were invited to partake of the wine as they wished, the vats would not be drained. But then, his ideas on drinking wine were drawn from his own family's experience. There, use of wine was limited to traditional religious observances; one small cup and only one cup of blessing for Kiddush and for Havdalah on the Sabbath, and one cup of blessing on festivals. Passover night was an exception, however. Then the traditional four cups for each individual would be enjoyed, as the Seder evening progressed, as blessings were recited.

His father had expanded the wine production, even opened an export enterprise, mainly to England. Two brothers had joined the business; he had been encouraged to choose a profession.

For eighteen months, Dreyfus had lived by hauling bricks and dirt, digging trenches, unloading cement sacks from railway cars and carrying them on his shoulder to construction sites. Finally, the infirmary needed a replacement physician.

He had not been the only doctor then performing hard labor. But, as the art of healing was not in high demand in the kingdom of death, he was the only one called for service.

"It's not going to be painful, and your leg will heal in a matter of weeks." Smiling, he again took my hand in his.

I slept, almost slept. There were voices, hovering presences.

At length, I awakened, instinctively touched my left leg, heavily bandaged.

"Is there pain, Beril?"

He covered me with the blanket and ordered me to sleep.

Marching steps, a dream? No; the monotony came closer, became louder. I sat up, glanced out my window.

My fellows were returning to the barracks. They were sullen, exhausted. Tuesday I had been one of them, marching the same road morning and evening. I strained my eyes to see them well, all of them, a great multitude.

I saw no Moses, no Red Sea on the horizon.

First came Unit 25, men between twenty-five and thirty-five. Their steps were heavy, their eyes sapped of vitality.

In the distance dragged Unit 52, the cable unit, notorious for its extreme mortality rate, There, second to the left, was marching a shadow, Hersh Leib Meizels. My uncle. From Slotvina. An outstanding authority on both the Talmud and the Kabbalah. He didn't last.

A stream of cold sweat was running down my spine. My own unit was now passing in review. There they were, all but one.

How did they fare today? Did they miss me, note my absence?

The steps faded, the slaves were again inside the compound, behind the wire. For the first time I had the specific awareness that my window faced the road leading to and from the camp. Twice a day hence I would hear, would see those unfortunates tread that road, while I lay on my bed secure from death, discomposed by guilt.

By the third day I cherished my blessings. My leg was healing, I was getting more food than what was given on the outside, the dread and fear of each day had been reduced. Most precious of all was the exemption from life-draining labor.

On my fifth day, the sickroom barber was discharged, his injury sufficiently mended. He had been pushing a wagon of iron beams; one had fallen from the load, striking a glancing blow on his right eye.

A tall, ruddy man of about thirty-five, he had entered camp with his wife and three young children, had not heard of them since. How then could that man retain his ability to infuse others with optimism, never to utter a word despairing or negative?

The ancient stories say that at twilight, cast-out and rejected souls begin their nightly journey throughout the world in search of purification. Should such a soul encounter some act of kindness performed by one human being to another, a manifestation of love between husband and wife, an act of grace between mother and daughter, father and son, a measure of charity given one person by another, then the soul hurries back to heaven and presents the act of love or grace before the heavenly tribunal to show that goodness has not altogether perished from among the children of men. And thus, the world is granted a new lease on life, a new sun to emerge above the dark horizon, while the soul which brought salvation to the world is admitted into the sublime bosom of Creation from whence all souls emanate, to which all souls, rectified, return.

Should any of those graceless souls have chanced upon that barber, their return to the bosom of Creation would have been assured.

He, however, was returned to his iron beams, and I, I petitioned for the job of barber.

First with trepidation, then with increasing confidence, I entered upon my task. Suddenly, I was important in my own mind, as well as in the minds of others. I had a calling, a reason for living. I exercised special care not to pinch those who came to me.

I now received a second bowl of soup, frequently given to me from the bottom of the kettle. That extra portion was mine for six weeks.

23

Rosh Hashanah

ON 18 SEPTEMBER my hospital barracks received word that all those who were making unsatisfactory progress toward recovery would be moved, to a better hospital. The announcement came on the first day of Rosh Hashanah; the selection would occur on the following, the second day of the Jewish new year.

As the sun was bestowing its last rays, many of the sick and injured gathered in one corner of the barracks. We prepared for prayer; did it matter that prayer was forbidden, that we had no prayer books? We made ready to receive the new year.

Each man labored to temper his urge to raise his voice as seldom before; the hospital staff seemed sympathetic to our tradition, others outside might not have been so gracious. We tried, did not always contain our sobbing and bitter outcry.

> Grant honor, Lord, to Your people, glory to those who revere You, hope to those who seek You, and confidence to those who await You.

Honor? glory? Could the ensuing year be any less abominable than the past several?

> Then will the righteous be glad, the upright rejoice, the pious celebrate in song. When You remove the tyranny of arrogance from the earth, evil will be silenced, all wickedness will vanish like smoke.

When had humankind ever exhibited arrogance more vicious than that now rampant in every corner of the world? How did it come to pass that so few were engaged in the work of Creation, so many reveling in the muck of destruction?

On the morning of the second day, I made a special point of

watching the imprisoned multitude forced out to expend another bit
of life in order that a war machine might live.

Had they said their prayers last night?

Those of us in the hospital gathered again in the corner. Each of us
delved into his heart, recalling prayers, recovering the order of
service.

A man of forty took his turn. In the midst of a deep silence, he gave
voice; melodious and clear he chanted.

> On Rosh Hashanah it is written, and on Yom Kippur it is sealed. How
> many shall leave this world and how many shall be born into it. Who
> shall live and who shall die. Who shall perish by fire and who by water;
> who by sword and who by beast, who by hunger and who by thirst,
> who by strangling and who by stoning. Who shall be at peace and who
> shall be tormented . . .

In childhood, I had imagined that heavenly scene. The Holy One,
praised be He, sitting on the throne of justice and flanked by cohorts
of angels, opens the book of mankind, leafs through its mammoth
pages. Leafing, He pronouces judgment on His creatures. His judg-
ments always mitigated by mercy, He signs and seals the destinies of
all His children for the coming year.

We continued our service. Although we had no shofar, we believed our prayers would be heard even without the customary
sounding of the ram's horn.

> The great shofar is sounded. A still, small voice is heard. This day even
> angels are alarmed, seized with fear and trembling as they declare:
> "The day of judgment is here!" . . . This day all who walk the earth pass
> before You as a flock of sheep. Like a shepherd who gathers his flock,
> bringing them under his staff, You bring everything that lives before
> You for review. You determine the life and decree the destiny of every
> creature . . .

Our cantor's voice broke, he fell with his face to the floor. We froze
in our places. Morning prayers had ended. On that Rosh Hashanah
we did not wish each other *L'shanah tovah tikatev v'taihatem*, "May
you be inscribed and sealed for a good year." We did not go home for
apples and honey.

I made my way, somehow, back to my bed, back to Szatmár.

For the entire summer, only Shiele and I had been home, studying at cheder. Our three older brothers were away at yeshivas. Two weeks before Rosh Hashanah, mother grew eager to embrace her long-absent sons, to consider how much they had grown, how much Torah they had acquired. Father tried to conceal his joy. It did not behoove a serious man, a scholar, to reveal deep sentiments. He barely succeeded. Shiele and I wanted to hear more of yeshiva life.

Finally, they were with us once again.

While mother prepared the holiday meal, we six, father and sons, walked to our synagogue ten blocks away. Going there, we met families walking to their synagogues, the synagogues on our side of town. We exchanged hurried greetings; no one wanted to be late for services.

Afterwards, everyone rushed homeward. We brought with us two guests, those who could not make it to their own homes for the new year. Mother was ready, the table set with wine, challot, apples, and honey. Our small lodgings almost exploded with—

Achtung!

His voice was more awesome than the clarion notes of the shofar.

Already we sat naked on our beds. The SS physician was handed a file of charts, our medical histories and prognoses. In thirty minutes, that man granted life or death to nearly as many patients, each one having passed, in fear and nakedness, before him. He was casual, indifferent. Could he have been otherwise?

The first part was over. He left with our charts in his briefcase, our futures undisclosed.

We retreated, each of us, behind invisible walls. No one spoke. The staff acted busy. Our chief physician asked, "What's the matter? Tomorrow some of you will be transported to a hospital where conditions and facilities—"

Next morning, directly at eight o'clock, a military truck pulled up outside our barracks. An SS officer came in, pulled out some charts, read off some numbers.

Those numbers left our congregation, went off to join one infinitely larger.

Toward the end of the day, each surviving inmate recovered at least part of his sense of self. Deep inside, most rejoiced in life, in having been granted at least some portion of the new year.

I announced it was time for haircuts. Immediately, an unusually large group formed around my barber chair. Few wished to be left alone. We talked, but not about yesterday, not about the morning just past.

Several days later, I was surveying the world outside my window. A number of young men and women, walking in pairs, came into view. All were dressed uniquely; they talked, occasionally laughed.

Did the stink of this place cause them no nausea? Did they not mind the smoke shrouding the heavens?

Someone noted a rabbit at rest in a field. The group started to run, parted in several directions, pursued the fleeing creature.

It escaped. Laughing, they continued together toward wherever it was they had been going.

Every few days Dr. Dreyfus would check my leg, change the bandages. Always, he tried to raise my spirits by telling funny little stories; I remember none of them.

Story told, he would ask me of my parents, my brothers. Then he would sit quietly for a while.

Finally, he would talk again of days that once had been.

Once, after a prolonged silence, he stared, looking like someone just awakened from a heavy sleep.

"You know, Beril, when I was with my son for the last time, he looked much like you."

Another silence.

"You should have seen the hours he spent studying biology. Do you think he could become a fine doctor?"

Seldom did he mention his daughters; they had been too young.

24

The Children

Even Satan created no quittance
For a small child's blood.
Let the blood cleave the void
Split the bottomless pit
Eat away the dark
And rot the foundations of the putrifying earth.

—Chaim Nachman Bialik

STATISTICS SAY THAT in the Holocaust one and one-half million Jewish children were murdered by the Nazis.

A staggering and mind-baffling figure.

Yet that is all that it is, a figure. Any figure inevitably fades into insignificance when confronted with the frightened eyes, the helpless and terror-stricken cry of one single child when snatched from the arms of its mother, tossed about like vermin, condemned to destruction.

Were it possible to classify and measure the atrocities committed by the Nazis, their bestialities against the children would emerge at the top. The horrified images of those hapless victims remain unerasable.

And it was precisely those innocent souls that the Nazis turned into a target for their sadistic pleasures. For children, there was simply no hope. They were the most helpless, the most defenseless, and the least suspecting victims of the Holocaust.

Memories, sights, painful experiences, inevitably fade into oblivion, their impact diminishing with the passage of time. There are impressions of such magnitude, however, that they keep on tormenting one's mind regardless of the element of time. Nay, they grow, intensify, and are everpresent.

102

My recollection of the three-day journey by train from Szatmár to Auschwitz is not very lucid. I recall that experience in fragmentary, shadowy glimpses only. Yet one impression, which lasted for only a short moment, will stay with me for the rest of my life.

It was the third day of our journey. We hadn't had water since the day we left Szatmár. Inside our cramped boxcar there was hardly enough air to breathe. There were no toilet facilities; the stench was unbearable.

It was dark. I couldn't see their faces, although they were quite close to me. First, I heard the child in an almost whispering voice.

"Mommy, my tongue is very dry. Please, let me have some water."

The mother kissed her daughter and said to her softly:

"My dear Rochi, there is no water here on the train. Soon we shall get out of this train and you will have water."

About half an hour later, the child again asked for water. She was given the same answer. But now I heard depressed sobbing. It was the mother, not the child, who cried. Then, I heard Rochi's soft, caressing voice.

"Don't cry, Mother, please, don't. I shall not ask for water any more. I promise."

Rochi kept her promise. She did not ask for water for the rest of the journey.

In a few more hours our train arrived in Auschwitz. Rochi and all the other children were taken to the gas showers. She had not been granted her last wish.

Soon after arrival I found myself in the selection line. People were directed either to the left or to the right. The human dregs moved on swiftly. Without even noticing I lost both father and mother, and Shiele. I was alone. They had been swallowed up by the moving mass.

In front of me, there was a couple of about forty years old and their eight- or nine-year-old son. Father and mother had been directed in opposite directions, one to the right, the other to the left. For some inexplicable reason, the child had not been ordered where to go. Taking his destiny in his own hands, the child turned to go with his mother. Then, somewhat hesitatingly, he retracted and headed toward where his father was standing, then vice versa. It was obvious that the youngster couldn't make up his mind. He was desperate. For a moment the line halted. Poor soul! He thought it was up to him to make the decision.

It must have been that the SS officer in charge had intentionally concocted the spectacle for reasons of self-gratification, or in order to add torment to the victim's anguish.

After a minute or two of passively watching, the SS officer hit the father with his billy, ordering him to move on. He kicked the bewildered boy with his boot, shoving him toward where his mother was standing. The line resumed its movement.

Whether a youth was immediately condemned or temporarily assigned for work hinged on a variety of factors. Was he short or tall, lean or well-built? Was he smiling or sullen, well-dressed or shabby? Was the SS inspector in a good or bad mood? What were the manpower requirements on that specific day?

Since the entire process of decision-making concerning an individual lasted only for a split second, arbitrariness inevitably played a major role in the life-and-death decision. That was especially true in borderline cases. Children between the ages of fourteen and fifteen were such borderlines. Anyone younger than that had almost no chance. Yet there is always an exception to the rule. Imre Grosinger of Mihályfalva was one such exception.

Emanuel and Ilona Grosinger traced their roots to four generations of parents and grandparents who had lived in the Mihályfalva area. Emanuel, a livestock dealer, would travel through the many villages surrounding Mihályfalva buying sheep and cattle from the peasants. Honest and of impeccable integrity, he had established throughout the years not only sound business contacts but friendly relations as well.

Well rooted in their local community, respected by townspeople and villagers alike, Emanuel and his wife Ilona had good reason to feel satisfied with their lot.

In their home, Jewish traditions and values were cherished and lived by. All of their three sons had been given a sound Jewish education. A practical man, Emanuel Grosinger had decided to endow his children with a fine secular education as well. When Sanyi and Laci, the two older sons, reached the age of twelve, their father took them to Nagyvárad and enrolled them in the local Jewish middle school.

The Kecskeméti Lipót School was one of the finest private schools in the country. Its founder and mentor, Rabbi Dr. Lipót Kecskeméti, was a fervent Magyar nationalist and patriot. He had preached loyalty to Hungarian nationalism and culture even when Nagyvárad was under Romanian dominion. Vehemently opposed to Zionism, he constantly called upon his liberal Neologist co-religionists to fully embrace Hungarian culture and civilization.

Fortunately for the rabbi, he did not live long enough to see his city "liberated" by the Hungarian military and his congregants carried away to Auschwitz in sealed boxcars.

In the autumn of the year 1943, at the age of twelve, it was the turn of Imre, the youngest of the three Grosinger brothers, to be taken to the Kecskeméti Lipót School. His two older brothers had by that time already been drafted into the notorious forced-labor brigades of the Hungarian military. Official and mob Jew-baiting were already rampant throughout the country. Yet Emanuel Grosinger was determined to continue the family tradition. Nagyvárad was, after all, only one hour's train ride from Mihályfalva. Besides, the Grosingers had friends there who would be closely watching both the young student and political developments.

Uncertainties and turbulent times were by no means a novelty to the Jewish people, Emanuel would argue with his wife. They certainly were not reason enough to deprive Imre of a good education. So father and son made the traditional trip to the big city.

Young Imre was quite impressed by the tall buildings, the elegant and spacious stores, and the broad paved streets. No more would he have to shake the sand out of his shoes as he was wont to do in Mihályfalva. Everything was unlike what he had been accustomed to in his hometown. He was especially attracted to the colorful streetcars running through the middle of the city. His greatest challenge, though, was meeting new friends, both from Nagyvárad and from other towns, who had come to study in the same school. To this experience he looked forward with eagerness.

Before long, Imre had settled down in his new environment, determined to make good grades, to live up to his parents' expectations.

But not for long.

On March 18, 1944, the Hungarian regent, Miklós Horthy, was meeting with Hitler at Schloss Klessheim at the urgent request of the Führer. Hitler had become exceedingly nervous about Prime Minister Miklós Kállay's secret attempts to extricate Hungary from its disastrous alliance with Germany. Even while the meeting was in progress, German occupation troops were marching toward the Hungarian borders. The dramatic events that quickly followed not only sealed the end of Hungary's independence but also doomed to destruction the majority of Hungarian Jewry, including Emanuel and Ilona Grosinger. For among the invading German forces there were also Adolf Eichmann's *Einsatzgruppen*, special SS units entrusted with the task of the Final Solution.

At that time, Imre would have shrugged his shoulders had anyone mentioned to him such strange words as *Einsatzgruppen*, *Eichmann*, and *Final Solution*. He had certainly sensed the anxieties shared by the Jewish community. He had sensed that extraordinary events were happening. Yet he was sure things would eventually straighten out, as they always did. After all, when had everything ever run smoothly for the Jews? They always had to sail rough seas, to weather turbulent storms, but in the final analysis they always made it. Why should this time be different?

Toward the end of March, the Germans marched into Nagyvárad. Imre did not, as yet, suspect that this move would have profound consequences not only on his studies but on his entire life.

The first anti-Jewish act of the Germans in Nagyvárad was the confiscation of the local Jewish hospital. All of the patients in this modern facility, the pride of the Jewish community, had to be evacuated within two days so that it could be converted into a German military hospital.

Sometime in April, Imre came down with a strep throat. He had a high fever and experienced pain in swallowing. When his case was diagnosed as scarlet fever, he was taken to a hospital for communicable diseases.

Scarlet fever was not generally considered dangerous. Yet for the Grosinger family, Imre's illness had far-reaching consequences.

At the very same time that Imre fell ill, the Final Solution mechanism was set in full motion throughout Hungary. The experience and the efficiency accumulated in Europe's other occupied countries were being put to full use at this final stage of the Final Solution. After all, was not the Jewish situation in Hungary an anachronism? At a time when most of Europe's Jews had already been gassed and burned, close to one million Jews in Hungary were still enjoying relative normalcy.

The months of April, May and June witnessed the return to Hungary of scenes from prehistoric days, coupled with the worst barbarities of medievalism, executed with the scientific precision of the modern technological era. The apparition of Attila was hovering over Hungary.

An enormous movement of people was set in motion. Entire populations of villages, towns, and cities were suddenly uprooted as if by an avalanche. Throughout the roads and railways of Hungary more than half a million Jews—men, women, children, some sick and crippled—were driven from their homes, robbed of their possessions, deprived of their elemental dignity, even of their very human image.

They had been condemned to destruction.

A feverish undertaking of construction overtook all of Hungary. Ghettos for the Jews were popping up at full speed in all of the country's larger cities. Children were expelled from their schools, physicians dismissed from hospitals; clerks, merchants, artisans, workers all had to stop whatever they were doing and go into the ghetto. An entire nation, with only few exceptions, had gone mad in a frantic witch-hunt. True, there was the irresistible temptation of looting, appropriation, and dispossession. Yet that does not explain it all. Wisliceny, one of Eichmann's chief lieutenants in Hungary, confessed: "The Hungarians really seem to be the offspring of the Huns. Without them, we would never have succeeded like this."

At his postwar trial in Budapest, General Ferencz Szombathelyi chief of the Hungarian General Staff during the war and one of Hungary's main war criminals, made the following revealing confession: "The Jewish question had a catastrophic effect upon the armed forces. Cruelty became love for the Fatherland; atrocities became acts of heroism; corruption was transformed into virtue. We simply could not understand the events. There emerged two types of decency; one was applied to the Jews against whom any action was permissible."

Mihályfalva did not have enough Jews to justify the establishment of a ghetto in the city. Its seventeen hundred Jewish inhabitants were driven to a temporary site of concentration from where they would then be taken by train to the ghetto of Nagyvárad.

Emanuel and Ilona Grosinger could have escaped deportation. A gentile friend of theirs in one of the smaller villages offered them shelter and a hiding place for the duration of the war. But Imre was in Nagyvárad in the hospital. There was no way to bring him home. How could they go into hiding and abandon their youngest child? They decided to go with the rest of the Jews into the ghetto.

In Nagyvárad the authorities had established two ghettos, a large ghetto for the twenty-seven thousand local Jews, and a smaller one for the approximately eight thousand Jews from Mihályfalva,

Margitta, Székelyhid, and many smaller towns and villages. This smaller ghetto for the provincial Jews was located at the Mezey Lumberyard.

Imre was still recuperating in the hospital from his scarlet fever.

One morning, the hospital's chief administrator came to see him. Putting on a facade of normalcy and civility, he exchanged a few conventionally polite sentences with the patient. Then, somewhat embarrassed and apologetically, he told the young patient he would have to leave the hospital. All the Jews of Nagyvárad and of the provinces as well, he informed Imre matter-of-factly, had already been rounded up and taken into the ghetto. It was in Imre's own best interest, the administrator said, to join the rest of the Jews.

For the last couple of days Imre had been feeling much better. He had no fever, and experienced no pain when swallowing. But now, following the administrator's short visit, Imre's entire body was thrown into a spasm of convulsions. He was sweating and shaking. He wasn't sure whether it was a recurrence of his illness or the news just conveyed to him that had caused his convulsions.

The door opened with a swift push. Two armed guards entered the room. In no polite words and without even the semblance of niceties, they urged Imre to quickly get dressed and follow them.

At that moment, Imre became an outcast, an undesirable, a non-person. He was no more under the protection of the law of human decency. The conventional civilities of polite society no longer applied to him.

In the ghetto Imre was reunited with his parents amidst tears of joy. There he also found all of his friends, the entire Jewish community of Mihályfalva. Ilona and Emanuel Grosinger now became convinced even more that they had made the right decision by not accepting the offer of a hiding place.

The Mezey Lumberyard was not exactly the best-suited place for human accommodation, certainly not for eight thousand people, many of whom were old, young children, and ill. The "living quarters" of the ghetto had only a roof; there were no walls or floor. Nor were there tolerable toilet facilities. There was not enough drinking water. Many had to sleep on the bare ground. At night it was quite cold.

The trapped prisoners tried to make some sense of what was happening to them, but they were at a complete loss. It just did not make any sense. Rather, everything seemed senseless, insane.

Deportation, Selection, Final Solution.

These fateful words had not yet become part of the vocabulary of the ghettoized Jews. No wonder they were at a loss to put some logic into the madness of an unfathomable world which had turned topsy-turvy.

Within ten days, all the thirty-five thousand Jews from both ghettos had arrived in Auschwitz.

Dazed and bewildered, Imre and his parents climbed out of the boxcar in which they had spent some five days. Imre's first glimpses caught sight of strange-looking, baldheaded people dressed in pajamas and running around. With a shy smile on his face he now apologetically confesses his ignorance of the past.

"I thought they were convalescing soldiers running about their daily exercises."

Even before he could set his mind in order he found himself in a rapidly moving line accompanied by shouts, shoving, clubbing. Then he saw his father moving in one direction while he and his mother were moving in the other.

"I cannot explain how that happened," Imre recalls the event with deep emotion. "I don't know why I began to run after my father. Everything happened so fast."

Imre, at that time, certainly knew nothing about selections. He had not yet learned the difference between being sent to the left or to the right. It must have been an intuition, a spur-of-the-moment decision, a Providential inspiration. That reflexive action of a built-in instinct for survival spelled for Imre the difference between death and life. He was fortunate, in addition, that the SS officer in charge did not notice him switching lines.

In a follow-up selection sometime later, he was, after all, separated from his father and shoved into a children's camp of about three thousand. Their numbers, however, kept on diminishing daily as a result of starvation, illness, and recurring selections.

Husky and well-built , Imre managed to pass all the selections and survive. Yet he still did not understand why he had been brought to this place called Birkenau. Nor did he comprehend what all the commotion was about, that is, what purpose the place served. The huge barracks, the multitudes of people being pushed around and counted, starved to death, selected over and over, all this simply didn't make sense to his childish perspective.

What especially made him wonder were the huge flames and the putrid odors ascending from a factory nearby. The building seemed to be the only one in the camp, except for the kitchens, that was producing something.

But what was it producing?

One day he found out.

To Imre's delight, following the many selections and separations from parents and friends, he discovered Gregory. This fourteen-year-old boy was the son of a dentist from Myhályfalva. He too had been separated from his parents on the day of their arrival. Imre and Gregory promised each other to stick together as long as possible. In Birkenau they performed various chores ordered by their kapo, always inventively maneuvering to stay together.

One morning, as the two were walking to one of their daily chores, they heard someone calling excitedly, "Gregory, Gregory!" They looked around and recognized Dr. Klein, the dentist, Gregory's father. He was calling to them from beyond a fence that separated the two camps.

An emotional reunion between father and son followed, but only in words. They could not touch each other, for the fence separated them. Both parties knew well that what they were doing was not permitted. They had to move fast to avoid being caught and severely punished.

"What are you doing over there, Father?"

"I am pulling out gold teeth, son."

"Gold teeth? From whom?"

"From the dead people."

"And how do those people die?"

"They are being gassed."

"Is it painful, Father, to be gassed?"

"I hope not."

"What are those flames that burn day and night?"

"That is the crematorium, my child. When the dentists have finished pulling out the gold teeth and the fillings, the bodies are burned."

There was a terrible silence, then a frightening scream. The two boys ran as quickly as they could. As they ran they heard the doctor's voice desperately calling to them: "Take care of each other, children, take care!"

It was thus, plain and simple, that Imre learned in a few minutes the meaning and the essence of Auschwitz. At that moment Imre came of age. He was no longer an innocent twelve-year-old boy. Now he started looking realistically at the planet called Birkenau.

Several weeks later, Dr. Klein was executed by the Germans but not because he had divulged the secret of the Final Solution to his son. Dr. Klein had belonged to a *Sonderkommando*, a special unit of prisoners chosen by the Nazis to work at the crematoria. In order to prevent any leakage to the outside world of the mass exterminations, the Germans would execute every several weeks the *Sonderkommando*, replacing them by new arrivals. When they realized that their own turn to be gassed was nearing, they planted dynamite in one of the ovens. The explosion which followed killed several of the SS guards. During the tumult that ensued, a large number of prisoners escaped, but they were later apprehended and executed. It was an act of supreme valor and defiance.

On January 18, 1945, Imre was put in an open boxcar and shipped from one camp to another. The Allied forces were advancing on all fronts, and the Germans did not know what to do with the prisoners whom they had not yet killed.

In the course of his macabre train ride, Imre saw death reign supreme. Many prisoners died of starvation, froze to death, or were shot. In a short time he was put into three of the notorious death camps: Gross-Rosen, Sachsenhausen, and Mauthausen.

In the course of those journeys he became separated from Gregory. Each new day was more hellish than the day before, and he felt his energies sapped to the breaking point.

In Mauthausen, his last camp, Imre had a race with time. He knew the American forces were not far away, but he wasn't sure his failing strength would sustain him until they arrived.

On the morning of May 6, Lieutenant Rosenberg of Chicago and a platoon of the U.S. Army entered Mauthausen. Shortly afterward, however, they left without giving any explanation.

It was only two days later, on May 8, that the main U.S. force in the area entered the camp and liberated its prisoners.

Imre was weak, but alive.

In retrospect, Imre did not mind that he had to wait for two more days. The date of May 8 held a very special meaning for him. It was his thirteenth birthday, his Bar Mitzvah day. He could never have dreamt that he would become Bar Mitzvah under such circumstances. Nor did he ever expect to get such a beautiful Bar Mitzvah gift from the U.S. Army, from the American people, a new lease on life.

Home in Mihályfalva, Imre found his two brothers, who had survived the horrors of the Hungarian labor brigades. He learned that of his extended family of twenty-eight, who had been taken to Auschwitz, only he and a cousin of his had survived. Not even one of his classmates, or of the class immediately higher than his, had survived.

In 1948, Imre arrived in the United States, where he was welcomed by an aunt and four uncles, all on his mother's side of the family.

In 1953, he enlisted in the U.S. Army and was subsequently stationed in Germany as part of the American occupation forces in that country.

"I fully sensed the queer twist of history," Imre admits. "Yet I harbored no hatred toward the German people," he adds. "I took great pleasure in serving my adopted country. I felt a deep sense of satisfaction at being able to 'repay' even a small measure of my debt to my liberators."

"After the war," Imre candidly confesses, "I had no faith in God. My faith had gone up in the flames of Birkenau; it had been buried beneath the ashes of the dead corpses of my cremated people. I just could not see how God and Auschwitz could coexist in the same universe."

Then, the transformation occurred.

It happened when Imre and his wife celebrated the twelfth birthday of their son Eric.

"As I looked at this tender boy, bone of my bone, flesh of my flesh, the full magnitude of my own life experience was forcefully impressed on me. It was then that I realized for the first time how young and tender I must have been at the age of twelve when my whole world was being torn asunder.

"With my two brothers now dead, it dawned on me that I was the only living branch of the Emanuel and Ilona Grosinger tree. I likewise realized that, in time, my son Eric would be the one to carry on the family name.

"As if in flashback, all the fateful happenings of my thirteenth year passed through my mind. The gymnasium, the hospital, reunion in the ghetto, moving trains, searing thirst, devouring hunger, selections, flames, gas, gold teeth, twisted faces. All fully presented themselves in a wild race, in a mixture of images and sequences.

"How was I able to go through all this hell and survive?

"I looked at Eric and saw myself. Then I remembered my Bar Mitzvah, the Bar Mitzvah that wasn't; Liberation Day, May 8. I looked at my wife and at our children, and a stream of love and of gratefulness flowed through my being.

"At that moment there remained no doubt in my mind that our son Eric would have his Bar Mitzvah celebration. He would continue to carry the traditions and the life-legacy of Emanuel and Ilona, his martyred grandparents.

"I am not yet fully reconciled with God. I still cannot grasp, let alone explain, the Holocaust; I never shall. Yet my newly won family and the rebirth of the Jewish people in its ancient homeland make life worth living, worth hoping."

25

A Normal Day in Buna

DURING MY CONFINEMENT in Auschwitz, I was a slave worker in the section of the camp complex known as Buna, where the I. G. Farben synthetic rubber plant was located.

The nights in Buna were quiet and private. Under the shield of the blanket and the cover of darkness, one was free to weave his dreams and to build worlds of his own making. It was of the utmost importance to sail freely on the wings of fantasy and imagination, to escape reality. I remember myself concentrated in both emotional and physical exercise to sever myself from the experiences of the day just past, and from the thoughts of what I might expect of the day about to dawn in just a few hours. It would have been too much to endure, too difficult to cope with. One day at a time was more than enough to see oneself through. Night was soothing, caressing, comforting.

I would turn myself from my right side to the left, and from the left to the right, in an effort to summon along visions, real and imaginary, from my past. At times, they would present themselves in profusion like a stream, competing and racing with one another. Some went back to the earliest days of childhood, recalling events and images unfamiliar to me while fully awake. Others appeared in their starkest reality, magnified and amplified, so as to cause utter joy and ecstasy. Such nights were endowed with divine grace. I wished them to last for eternity.

On other nights, I toyed with the angel of the future. Covering myself tightly with my blanket, I tried to shrink into nothingness, roving into the infinite expanses of worlds not as yet created, nevertheless real.

Once, I found myself in a very huge banquet hall with tables and

114

chairs made of pure sapphire. Invisible sources of light radiated brightness unlike anything earthly. Multitudes of guests, their countenances radiating joy and wisdom, were being served exotic delicacies in abundance, and red wine flowed from a river. A figure of royal stature girded with sword played the harp. I approached some of the guests and asked for food; they gave me generously and plentifully. I devoured what I had very quickly, and kept on asking for more food. Although the setting appeared to me painfully familiar, I could not remember where and when I had seen a familiar scene.

Not always was the angel of dreams so kind. At times, when the most blissful of scenes was in the midst of being woven, the colorful fabric would tear into shreds, leaving me outside in the cold, exposed and unprotected.

Once I saw myself carrying a heavy load of bricks, urged by a taskmaster's whip to speed up my pace. No matter how fast I endeavored to go, the whip lashed on my sore back. I began to run, breathing heavily under the enormous yoke, the taskmaster's whip still reaching me. Then a huge brick wall erected only the day before collapsed and fell on me and on my load. I shouted terribly. I didn't want to be buried alive and become part of the wall. Upon hearing my cries, the taskmaster hit me even harder until I fell down exhausted, unconscious.

In the morning, I felt a piercing pain in my right thigh. I thought I was imagining it. I felt the sore spot with my fingers. It was real and very painful. I looked at the spot and it was red. I couldn't figure out how an event that took place only in a dream would leave real traces on my flesh.

A few minutes later in the shower, my friend caught a glimpse of the red spot and remarked casually, "He really was hard on you." Startled, I asked him what he was talking about. He told me. In the middle of the night I had begun to shout very terribly, waking up the entire barracks. Then the block orderly came and struck me several times with his billy until I stopped shouting and started sobbing quietly. My friend comforted me by saying that he too sometimes experienced frightening dreams.

The days in Buna, by contrast, were very real, leaving no room for fantasy and dreams. All were woven from the same yarn—drab, insipid, listless. It didn't matter whether it was Monday, Wednesday, or Thursday, the routine was the same. Since none of us had a watch, and there were no calendars or newspapers in sight, time had, indeed, become a formless mass, lacking identity, just as we lacked one.

In order to survive the day, it was wise not to think about yesterday or contemplate the morrow. Constant alertness and scheming were of supreme importance. Carrying heavy loads of bricks and cement bags all day long could be too damaging to one's health. One had to keep his eyes open to see whether he could steal a few seconds without inviting the ire of his kapo or of a passing SS officer. Likewise, one had to alert himself to the proper moment when he could hide an empty cement bag on his body and carry it to camp after work. The paper, when wrapped around one's lean body in the winter, could preserve a few calories and spell the difference between life and death. Alas, from time to time, the SS would conduct body searches and confiscate such contraband, often rewarding the smuggler with a few lashes.

Food, or rather, hunger, was the most overriding concern. A gnawing sensation of being hungry was the constant companion of the Buna slave. One's mind had to be on constant alert for possible sources of supplemental food, although the chances were mostly nil.

In my labor kommando there were three or four teenagers. At noontime, after he had finished lunch, our kapo would order one of the teenagers to clean his bowl. He intentionally left some of the food, usually soup, in the dish. The lucky dishwasher would wipe the dish so clean with his fingers that it hardly needed any additional cleaning. Those who were not fortunate enough to be teenagers swallowed their saliva and looked aside dejected. The kapo, a German criminal, once ordered me to peel five raw potatoes for him, with the implicit understanding that I could keep the peels. I did not make a special effort to peel the potatoes thinly. At camp, outside the barracks, there was a pipe constantly emitting hot steam. I kept the peels under the steam until they softened. I had my most delicious meal for months.

Many kapos were sadistically inclined toward the slaves entrusted into their care, afflicting them with hardships and cruelties beyond the call of duty. I was fortunate to have one endowed with compassionate feelings. He certainly wasn't a Gandhi; yet considering the circumstances, he was a spark of light in the bleak darkness of night. I often wondered about his other life, that is, his life before he was confined to the concentration camp. Did he have a wife, children?

What most intrigued me was the type of crime he had committed out there, for which he was now serving concentration camp confinement. Did he have Jewish neighbors? Perhaps even Jewish friends? I could only guess the answers, since it was out of the question to try and engage in private conversation with one's kapo.

Besides hunger and hard labor, which plagued us every day of the year, we had another, no less ominous enemy to devastate us in the winter. In low temperature and with our poor garb, the cutting cold would pierce to the very marrow of our bones. Having to combat hunger, exhausting labor, and biting frost often just became too much to contend with, and many succumbed.

Sometimes, deep down in my heart, I hoped that the rumors I heard concerning the fate of our parents were true. I hoped that my father and mother did not have to go through this hell day after day. If destiny so decreed, wasn't it preferable to die only once, rather than die in daily installments?

Concerning Shiele, I hoped he was as fortunate as I was to have been assigned to a kapo in whom all humane sentiments had not been extinguished. Deep in my heart, though, I knew I was indulging in illusion and wishful thinking.

There was an inmate in our group who managed to keep track of the festivals and holidays. One cold October morning, just as we arrived at our place of work, he announced that it was Simchat Torah, the day Jews celebrate the conclusion of the annual cycle of Torah readings. This festival is one of the most joyous of Jewish holidays, one of its highlights being the reading of Moses' final blessing to the tribes of Israel. The atmosphere is both joyous and solemn. Moses' last words are repeated by the reader as many times as needed to call up to the Torah every person present and read to him at least three verses. As a result, these passages are more familiar to the average synagogue-goer than most other portions of the Torah.

At our noon break that day we sought out an inconspicuous site to celebrate Simchat Torah. We took turns reciting passages from Moses' blessing.

"The Lord came from Sinai; He shone upon them from Seir . . . lightning flashing at them from His right," said a man of about forty, his limbs trembling, eyes flashing.

The one next to him took over. He was much younger, about twenty-five, a follower of the Szatmárer Rebbe. He told us of a unique experience that had occurred when he celebrated Simchat Torah the year before with the Rebbe.

The large synagogue had been packed with more than a thousand Chassidim waiting for their leader to appear. When he came in to meet his Chassidim his face was aflame and his white beard like glittering silver. Holding high a scroll of the Torah in his hands, he danced for hours, running forth and back in ecstasy. The spirituality among the mesmerized worshippers was so intense that several of them fainted.

Some of the veteran Chassidim who had celebrated Simchat Torah with the Rebbe on previous occasions testified that never before had they seen him so absorbed and so disturbed. When he read the blessing for Reuben he repeated it many times very loudly and in a pleading tone. Did he have a foreboding of what was soon to happen to his Chassidim and to all Jews?

The young Chassid now recited Moses' words: "Let Reuben live and not die, though few be his numbers."

Caught up in a frenzy, he kept on reciting the verse over and over, each time emphasizing another word with prolonged concentration. There was no doubt in our minds as to what had prompted him to repeat this particular verse so many times.

Another one took his turn. He spoke of Levi, of his utter devotion to the service of the Lord. He concluded, "Bless, Lord, his substance, . . . smite through the loins of them that rise up against him, and of them that hate him."

Others spoke of Judah and of Benjamin. But then the signal was given that lunch hour was over, and we had to return to work. While walking, a slave still ventured to say: "The eternal God is our refuge, and He thrust out the enemy from before thee. And Israel dwelleth in safety, the fountain of Jacob alone. . . . Happy art thou, O Israel, who is like unto thee? A people saved by the Lord."

We dragged our tired bodies and sullen faces to the work stations. No one suspected in the slightest that something spectacular was awaiting us at camp on that day of Simchat Torah.

On our way back to the camp after work we noticed an unusual movement of SS troops, tense and heavily armed. They were heading toward our camp. Then we noticed that the labor units, instead of dispersing toward their respective barracks, were marched to the *Appell Platz*, the camp square where we gathered every morning for counting. This time, however, it was not for counting that we gathered, but to witness something morbid.

In the center of the *Appell Platz* there were three gallows, three ropes swinging in the cold breeze. I was to witness for the first time an execution by hanging. Not one, but three victims. My blood froze. My entire body shivered.

The band at the gate was still playing its selections of marching music. The last of the labor units shouted out their numbers and marched to join the rest of us. The reverberating tunes, the echoes of the marching steps, the nervous shouts of the kapos, the barking SS dogs, and the swinging ropes combined into an entity even the most daring surrealist could not have come up with.

The three victims, two in their twenties, one juvenile, were led toward the gallows. The first stars had already appeared in the sky. The cold autumn breeze sent a shiver into our bones, reminding us what to expect when winter came. We were ordered to look at the gallows and to witness the executions.

Everything was ready. A suffocating silence and helplessness paralyzed the slave mass. Then, piercing the terrible silence, sounds came from the direction of the gallows. Moments before the ropes were fastened around their necks, the victims spoke loudly words of encouragement to their fellow comrades and words of defiance to their tormentor-executioners, the Germans. Then they too were silent: three bodies swinging in the cold breeze, silhouetted by huge searchlights from the watchtowers.

That night I had nightmares. The youngest of the three was about my age. Never before had death presented itself to me so personally and so directly as on that night of Simchat Torah.

26

Only on Friday

YENÓ WAS OF short stature, his dark complexion highlighted by a pair of red, fleshy lips. His physical constitution was definitely not the blond, tall, Aryan type. Nor could he be defined as having a typical "Jewish look." He easily could have passed for a Greek or an Italian. I don't know whether Yenó had ever given thought to such speculation. What I do know is that even in that pit of misery called Buna, this approximately twenty-year-old Hungarian Jew was quite comfortable with, even proud of, his identity. How he ended up in a German concentration camp rather than a Hungarian forced-labor brigade had never been clarified to me. Perhaps, he suffered from some physical disability which disqualified him for military service, but not for extermination camp.

To work with Yenó in the same kommando was no mere coincidence. It was a rare privilege. It may have been one of those blind chance factors which eventually determined who would die and who would live; that is, who would end up in the chimney, and who would see himself a free man again.

In Buna, smells had a tremendous hold on the slave population. Even today, some forty years later, whenever I happen to pass near a construction site where tar is being heated or poured on the road, the sharp odor of that black mass and the accompanying smoke strikes my nostrils in a peculiar way. It revives in me scenes and associations forever indelible. In Buna I learned that the sense of smell is the most powerful among all the senses we possess.

As a result of the extremely crowded conditions inside the Buna camp, it was impossible to escape the evil odors of sweat, breath, and the dirty rags the slaves used for wrapping their feet and their bodies. The primitive open-pit latrines and the sharp chemicals spread over them could knock one unconscious on first impact. The cheap, makeshift cigarettes made of various herbs and wrapped in newsprint that some of the prisoners smoked could induce in others headache and vomiting. Yet the most agonizing and tantalizing smells one had to endure in Buna, both in the camp and at work, were those that came from the various kitchens and food-distribution centers. They taxed and tormented our nostrils and nerves to the point of explosion.

When my kommando was not assigned to carry bricks and cement bags, we were put into a deep pit where we had to boil tar and smear it on huge container-tanks about to be buried deep in the ground. While the depth of the pit somewhat protected us in the winter from the raging winds, this advantage was more than nullified by the mud and the icy water accumulated in the pit, seeping and soaking into our shoes, feet, and trousers. Besides, the pits were dangerous places in which to work. When the supporting earth was muddy, soaked with water, but not yet frozen, a huge chunk of earth would tear away and cover some of the prisoners, injuring or burying them alive. In one such pit I worked with Yenó and three other prisoners. We were part of a larger kommando that numbered some fifty slaves.

Yenó had had no official appointment of any kind. He was an ordinary slave like the rest of us. Yet from the first day we began working together, he was acknowledged by the rest of our small group not only as a friend but as a kind of leader. One simply felt good being in his company. No matter how oppressive things were, Yenó exhibited a positive attitude, trying to infect us with his optimism. He liked to listen to our stories of the past, and was eager to share with us his life-experiences.

Yenó was the product of an assimilated family from a small town near Debrecen. He first found out about his Jewishness not at home, but at school. Once, in the midst of a heated quarrel, one of his classmates shouted at him, "*te Zsidó,*" "You Jew!" When he asked for an explanation at home, his parents dismissed the entire incident as "children's talk," telling Yenó that while he was, indeed, of Jewish ancestry, they were now Magyars, and that was all that mattered. From that day on, Yenó told us, he became an introvert, staying away from his classmates, feeling like a stranger among them.

At the age of fourteen, when Yenó traveled to Debrecen to attend high school, he discovered something he had never heard of before. This new discovery would eventually entirely revolutionize his thinking. By chance, he met some youngsters who told him they were Jewish and members of a Zionist youth organization. The novelty of Hungarian Jews being able to nurture nationalistic sentiments other than Hungarian greatly fascinated and agitated him. He attended one of the meetings, where words were spoken such as he had never heard at home. The words *Zion, chalutz, kibbutz, aliyah,* sounded in his ears like music from a distant world. He still had some difficulty in putting things in order, in their proper sequence, yet he felt a sensation of great discovery. His self-esteem as a Jew immensely improved. He attended subsequent meetings whenever he could.

At home, when he enthusiastically shared his discovery with his parents, his father angrily dismissed the entire Zionist idea as dangerous and sheer nonsense. He even refused to intelligently discuss it with his perplexed son. Being a loyal son and a patriotic Hungarian nationalist, Yenó did not join the organization, as his friends would have liked him to do. Yet he maintained his contacts with his newly found Jewish friends, and, from time to time, attended their meetings, to which he became ever more attracted.

On March 18, 1944, Yenó was on a business trip to Budapest on behalf of his father's wholesale grain firm. It was also the day the Germans invaded Hungary. He hurried home to be with his family and see what the future would hold in store for them. In April, Yenó and his parents sewed yellow stars on their garments to comply with the new regulations. For three days none of the three—Yenó was an only child—left their home; they could not suffer the shame and humiliation of being seen by their gentile neighbors marked as Jews. In May, Yenó and his family were taken to the ghetto, and subsequently they were deported to Auschwitz.

Yenó told us that during those three days of seclusion, the darkest and most frightful in his entire life, his father openly discussed the merits and the mechanics of suicide for the entire family. Yet each time the discussion tilted toward that solution, his father would emerge with new hope. He would try to convince himself and his family that this whole tragedy must be a terrible mistake. There must have been a mix-up in orders, in authority, or in both, a mix-up which would soon be cleared up and rectified.

In Auschwitz, both of Yenó's parents were directed to the left. Yenó did not know any Hebrew; nor was he familiar in the slightest with Jewish observance or ritual. Yet at Buna he underwent a total metamorphosis. Sure, Buna was not the ideal place for theological discussions, nor for experimentation in religious practice. Yet Yenó made a concentrated effort to find out more about his newly found religion. It may be said with all certainty that he was transformed into a *baal teshuvah*, a penitent, one who returns to his origins, to his roots. Knowing that I had been a yeshiva student, he asked me to teach him some of the most simple prayers and the blessings over water and bread.

It was Friday afternoon. The five of us were pouring boiling tar on one of the huge container-tanks, hungry, and shivering from the cutting cold. That day it was not my turn at lunch to clean the kapo's bowl. The Buna soup we had been served for lunch was extraordinarily tasteless and watery. My shoes, feet, and trousers were soaked with mud and icy water. There was a gnawing depression on everyone's face. We all knew it and felt it. There was no need for articulation.

Then Yenó spoke. Never before had we heard him speak that way. His eyes were aglow, his thick lips redder than ever, his voice trembling.

"It was on this day, on Friday," Yenó started his exhortation, "that God created man and put him into the Garden of Eden to enjoy life. God did not create man to suffer, nor did He create him to inflict suffering on other human beings, even not on animals. What is happening here in Buna and in other places is a terrible test. God is testing us, His children, to see how we respond to such a challenge. God wants to see whether we are able to preserve His divine image invested in us even here in Buna."

He went on for several more minutes, then abruptly stopped. It was obvious he had not yet finished what he had to say, he was waiting for a reaction from us. No reaction came forth, however. We all stood astounded and silent. Yenó resumed his sermon, lecture, or exhortation.

"Why, why did God do this to us? Have we sinned so terribly that we deserve such devastating punishment? Why is He always after us, while others get off with nothing?"

There was no doubt in our minds that Yenó was experiencing a deeply agonizing soul-searching. It was obvious that he intended to exonerate God of any wrongdoing, to give Him a clean record; yet the evidence was too overwhelming, too outcrying.

Following some minutes of silence came his surprising pronouncement.

"All that we are now suffering is deserved punishment. Herzl tried to awaken the Jews to go back to our own land from whence we had been driven out many centuries ago. Did we listen to him? No, we did not listen. Did we take him seriously? No, we did not! Did we take our prayers seriously? Thrice a day we turned in our prayers to Jerusalem, but that was as far as we were willing to go. We prayed to God that He return in mercy to Zion, yet we did not try hard enough to go there. Wasn't that enough to make God wrathful? Now here, we are suffering the consequences of our own folly."

The hour was close to sundown. Soon the siren would herald the end of another working day in Buna. This knowledge by itself somewhat lifted our sagging and dejected spirits. But this Friday was not destined to end as any other ordinary day. Yenó was holding still another surprise for us up his sleeve, or rather, in a mysterious package hidden under a board.

Solemnly and carefully he freed the package from beneath the board. Unwrapping its contents from the many layers of newspaper—eyes aglow and face smiling—Yenó held out in front of us a whole loaf of bread. We all looked in amazement, in disbelief. It was not the familiar brick-shaped Buna bread we got as rations. This one was a round civilian bread, striking our nostrils with a thousand and one associations of homebaked bread, challot, and cake. Was it a mirage? No, it seemed quite real. But where did he get it, and how? Such questions one did not ask at Buna, even not of his best friend. What was of more pressing interest to us was what he was going to do with it.

Yenó softly asked all of us to lay down our tools. Without questioning him we immediately obeyed. We would obey anything coming from a man who was holding a whole loaf of bread in his hands. He told us he was about to recite the Kiddush over the one loaf of bread, although he would have preferred to recite it over a cup of wine, or at least over two loaves as required by custom. No one laughed at this sad joke. In broken Hebrew, mixed with Hungarian, Yenó chanted the Kiddush. We listened in awe. Cutting open the bread with his sharp knife, he put one half of the loaf into his pocket and divided the other half into five pieces, handing a piece to each coworker. We remained speechless. In Buna, some people, as a matter of survival, stole bread and anything else they could. Yenó was giving away bread to others.

At that moment, Friday before sunset, I felt the wings of the

Shabbat angels touching me with grace. Deep in the pit of misery and mud a spark of light warmed up my sagging spirit, even made me forget for a moment my chilly bones and soaked feet.

Next Friday the same scene repeated itself, and the Friday after, again. Where he got a fresh loaf of bread every Friday was a question nobody asked. Was it a result of his inventive mind? Perhaps. Did he have contacts with civilians? Maybe. Was it one of those miracles children's legends are woven of? Who knows? He did not share this secret of his with us.

In December, I do not remember what day or week, there was an air raid on Buna. We were just about to be dismissed from work before sunset. Many bombs fell in the area where thousands of slaves lay on the frozen ground without shelter, desperately trying not to be hit. Some were killed, more were wounded. When the bombers left and we assembled for counting, Yenó was missing. The search team dispatched by the kapo came back with his dead body. He had incurred a direct hit. We carried his body back to camp in a stretcher to be counted by the Germans, so that our tally would be complete.

The prevailing rule at Buna read: It doesn't count whether you are alive or dead. But whether you are alive or dead, you must be counted.

Next Friday before sunset, the four of us instinctively put down our tools. We stood frozen for a moment and wept. Kiddush was not chanted that Friday, nor blessings pronounced. Small slices of bread were not handed out. We welcomed the Sabbath in sadness and in mourning. On that Sabbath Eve we felt abandoned and let down.

It occurred to me that the Sabbath angels wept and mourned with us, their wings clipped, their grace withdrawn.

27

Red Carpet (A Holocaust Midrash)

TINY SNOW FLAKES filled the horizon. Like brilliant stars they kept on coming in array. The telephone and electrical wires were glimmering white from millions of shiny parachutes. All the trees on the horizon had enveloped themselves in pure white prayer shawls, waving forth and back as if in prayer. Our barbed-wire fence too was festively dressed, all pure white. Only some stray birds skipping from wire to wire and leaping from branch to branch disturbed the perfect harmony of all-out white brilliance. The sight of those tiny creatures had often made me wonder how they survived the severe cold, and where they found food in the cold winter to nourish their bodies.

That winter morning in Buna was unique in the annals of Creation. It was a day by itself, not reckoned among, and unlike, the other days that ever were or will be. It was as if time stood still. It was the eighteenth day of January in the year 1945.

Already during the days and nights of late December and early January, movements of troops, military vehicles, and artillery could be noticed on the roads around the camp. There was also a noticeable change in the countenances and behavior of the SS troops who guarded us. They showed nervousness and seemed to be anticipating something. There was no change, however, in our work routine, except for the almost daily air raids. Howling sirens piercing the air followed by overflying aircraft had become commonplace. At such times, the civilians in the area were ordered into nearby shelters. We, the *Häftlings*, were not allowed into the shelters; we had to stay outside exposed to the bombs. During one of the raids, three of our inmates were hit by shrapnel and killed. When our day's work ended we were ordered to carry the three bodies on stretchers into the camp so that they might be counted together with the living. We had to return to camp our numbers undiminished.

On January 18, 1945, we did not report to work. All of the ten thousand forced-laborers remained in the camp. It was an unusual sight. Rumors filled the air and competed with one another. "The Russians are coming!" "The Americans are coming!" The various rumors differed as to whether the liberating armies were ten, twenty, or fifty kilometers away, whether it was a matter of a day, three days, or a week. But the entire prisoner body shared the inevitable conviction that very soon we would be free.

All day long we strolled around in the camp, disregarding altogether the cutting cold, speculating aloud about what the next hour would hold for us. Deep in our hearts we looked down on the SS guards stationed in the watchtowers all around the camp—we were convinced that their hour of reckoning was at hand.

Soft, tender snowflakes kept on coming down all day long, gently caressing our faces. As soon as they touched the ground, they were trampled and mutilated by multitudes of feet strolling forth and back. An incomprehensible sensation of festivity seemed to have permeated the camp. The very leisurely and relaxed atmosphere and high expectations had combined together and created that sensation. I was tempted to build a snowman, but the snow was too soft and melted away on contact. The camp was so jammed with people radiating heat that we all ignored the cutting January frost.

Another day came to my mind, a sunny September day when I had remained in the camp on account of my limping foot. But, then, that day had been real, accountable for, although somewhat different. I was the only prisoner to remain in camp; everyone else went to work, and I remained in camp for a good reason, for a purpose. But this day, the eighteenth day of January, was unusual, not accounted for, purposeless, as if torn out of the calendar, a day in which time stood still.

An alarming siren split the air, bringing our aimless wandering about to a sudden halt. Everyone froze on his feet. It was not an air raid. The familiar deep voice of our *Lagerälteste* was speaking to us from a loudspeaker.

I had known the camp commander from the first day I came to Buna. It was all but impossible not to be impressed by his towering figure from first sight. The green triangle affixed on his lapel, indicating his criminal background, was a perfect match to his deep, dark-green penetrating eyes. A German, perhaps the tallest person in the camp, he had a large head resting on well-built heavy shoulders. Even without the use of a microphone, his normal voice would carry quite far. I cannot remember ever having seen him without his thick rubber truncheon and his enormous German shepherd dog. To be treated by either would be such a memorable experience that no one had a desire for it. Seldom did he use his rubber truncheon; yet when he did, the results were quick and quite visible. Whether on mornings before work or evenings after returning from work, his imposing figure was always visible. Yet in all honesty it cannot be said that he was cruel, even bad. After all, he too was only a *Häftling* and constantly scrutinized by the SS. At heart he may even have been a compassionate man. For children, especially, he had a warm spot reserved in his heart, showing it whenever possible.

As his words to the prisoners now came through the loudspeaker, a slight change could be discerned in his voice. His efforts to the contrary notwithstanding, his voice cracked now and again. In spite of his concerted attempt to speak in a businesslike and matter-of-fact tone, he failed to conceal the agitation of his emotions. Instead of the usual voice of unchallenged authority, now it was that of the captain of a sinking ship. "In two more hours, as soon as it is dark, we shall be leaving this camp for an unspecified destination." The impact of these few words was enormous; everyone froze in his place. "To an unspecified destination": the words were ominous and chilled the very marrow of our cold bones. Instinctively there came to my mind similar words spoken on another occasion: the sick inmates selected at the infirmary were to be taken to "a place where better medical treatment was available." Now, all of us were to be taken to "an unspecified destination."

The *Lagerälteste*, his composure somewhat regained, his voice steady, went on, relating to us orders for the following two hours. At that time, at five o'clock, his kingdom would come to an end, his destiny, as yet, unspecified.

He told us that as soon as his orders were concluded, all clothing and shoe supply depots would be open. Anyone with torn or worn-out shoes or garb should present himself at one of the depots and replace the undesirable articles. Blankets too would be issued upon request for anyone who might want to wrap himself with one on the march. Each prisoner would also be given half a loaf of bread. Exactly at five o'clock all prisoners must present themselves at the

Appell Platz for a final count before the march began. Anyone found in the barracks after five would be shot.

My mind worked quickly. If there were some ominous plans concerning our lives, why would they even bother taking so many people someplace else? Wouldn't it be much simpler to finish us off right here and now? Besides, why would they bother supplying us with clothing, blankets, shoes, and bread if—? Certainly, there was ample room for arguments to the contrary too. One such argument, for example, could have been that all we had just heard from the camp commander was only a ruse in order to get us unawares, etc., etc. Yet such thoughts were immediately shoved aside. They were not compatible with our basic desire to live, to survive.

Now more than ever before I was determined to live, not to succumb, at least for several more hours. Soon the Russians or the Americans would come and take us by surprise. I clung to every hopeful sign to every hint, every rumor. The constant overflights of Allied aircraft coupled with the massive retreat on the ground of German troops and vehicles spoke louder than all the pessimistic calculations.

The two hours lasted for an eternity. Everyone made a supreme effort to equip himself with the best garb he could lay his hands on. The unusual generosity of the Germans in supplying us with these items was quite telling. It meant that our march would be arduous and lengthy. Only those who were well equipped would eventually make it to the "unspecified destination."

Ever since, I have often wondered what the Almighty and his heavenly host were engaged in on that dreadful, fateful, and unforgettable night between the eighteenth and nineteenth of January, in the year 1945. Did they look down at Buna, where an army of ten thousand of His faithful children was being led to torture by the waffen-SS? Did He say to His ministering angels, "Look down, My faithful servants, look down and see how My children are being led away by a cruel enemy. Look and see how steadfast in faith they are. None of them falters, look and see how eagerly and tenderly they support each other. They sustain the weary, strengthen the weak, share one another's burden."

Then the Almighty rose from His Throne of Glory. He leaned toward earth and listened. Motioning to the angels, He called on them to listen too. For a heavenly moment there was a freezing silence in the upper spheres. Neither angel nor cherub, not even the seraphim, moved or uttered a sound. The entire heavenly court directed its attention earthward, trying to catch a glimpse, a shred of a sound.

"What do you see there on earth, My faithful servants?"

It was the soft, tender, almost weeping voice of the Almighty that broke the unbearable silence.

Answered the angel Gabriel, patron of Israel: "O Lord of the universe, we see multitudes of Your children being led into the unknown by a brutal, relentless enemy. He does not favor the old, nor show compassion for the young."

"O Lord of the universe," broke in the archangel Metatron, "Your children are exhausted, starved, and emaciated. How will they survive the long, merciless march? How will they survive the biting frost, cutting to their very bones? You have handed them over to the worst of Hamans, the vilest of Amaleks."

At that time, the countenance of the Almighty appeared like a blazing torch. His eyes were two glowing coals, and from His nostrils came forth a storm of anger that shook the foundation of heaven, even the Throne of Glory.

Watching in awe and amazement, the angels saw God's two eyes darken and glow interchangeably. Now they glowed in dazzling glare, then looked like two extinguished coals. From His eyes, teardrops flowed onto the marble-white sapphire beneath His feet.

Then the Almighty spoke again.

"And now, My obedient heavenly servants. Listen, I beg you, listen carefully, and tell Me what My beloved children on earth are uttering at this moment."

All the heavenly court immediately attuned their ears earthward. Each angel and seraph exerted a supreme effort to catch and record the faintest whisper, sigh, or moan uttered by the children of Israel led away in torture.

A long silence followed. Then all the angels and seraphim unanimously exclaimed; "We can discern nothing of the nature of human utterance. All we can hear is their shortness of breath and their quick heartbeats."

The Almighty seemed both pleased and disappointed. Again He appealed to His angels to make one more effort and listen.

"They must be faint and of crushed spirit. They cannot utter words in a loud, articulate manner. Listen again, I beg you. Please, listen again, My ministering angels."

An even lengthier silence now followed. The heavenly host again exerted themselves at listening to the utterances of Israel.

"I can hear something," exclaimed Gabriel, pointing toward a spot in the vast distant darkness.

The entire heavenly court now listened and looked attentively in the direction pointed out by Gabriel. The voice was faint and crushed, yet not inaudible. Gradually, it became distinct and clear.

"*Shema Yisrael* . . . Hear, O Israel, the Lord is our God; He is One."

The voice reached its crescendo with the word "One," then fell silent. A purple-red spot appeared in the white snow. First, its size was not larger than a small phylactery. Weaving itself in all directions, the red spot expanded and grew into the size and shape of a tallit—a prayer shawl.

The angels looked on in amazement as a beautiful red carpet unfolded on the crystal-white snow. The carpet was perfect, symmetric, and flawless. Only, there was a tiny black hole at its heart.

Two white-winged, child-faced cherubim gently glided earthward. Heading toward the red carpet, they picked it up, and with reverential homage carried it heavenward.

It is believed that on the day King Messiah makes his appearance to redeem the remnants of Israel, this carpet will be the banner foretold by Isaiah: "He will raise a signal to the nations, and will gather the outcasts of Israel, and the scattered daughters of Judah will He assemble."

On that day, the Almighty will show the nations the red carpet with the tiny black hole at its heart. He will say to them: "See, I have scattered My people among you to spread My word and My teachings. Look, how you have dealt with them. Now, since you have misused My trust, I order you, free My people, and help them return to their inheritance in Zion and rebuild it."

The Almighty, eyes and face aglow, stretched forth his arms and received one more martyr. He placed his soul in the chamber into which neither angel nor seraph is admitted. That chamber, adjacent to the Throne of Glory, is reserved solely for the souls of martyrs who have died for the sake of sanctifying the name of the Almighty.

From one of the nearby villages the crow of a cock was heard.

It was midnight.

28

The Great March

THE SUN'S LAST rays began withdrawing westwards; the first stars made their early appearance around a pale moon. In the beginning they appeared slowly, hesitantly; then, in quick succession, they dotted the dark horizon with millions of brilliant silvery specks. A huge canopy of black velvet decorated with myriads of silvery stars began enveloping and sheltering a wounded and tired universe.

The moon above our heads moving along with us slowly and gently was by no means strange to me. I used to watch the moon every month as it was growing from a hardly visible crescent into a full-faced mature being. At such a time I loved to join the worshippers assembled at the synagogue courtyard for the monthly ceremony of the Blessing of the Moon. Unlike other prayers, this one took place outdoors, under the open sky. This monthly ceremony used to fascinate me as a child, alerting me to the natural phenomenon of the changing phases of the moon. There was something in the moon symbolic to my people. They are constantly being diminished, yet always regenerate and revitalize.

On that night of the Great March I recalled the words from the Blessing of the Moon ceremony.

> They are glad and happy to do the will of their Creator who ordered the moon to renew itself as a glorious crown over those He sustaineth. They, likewise, will be regenerated in the future.

I remembered how I loved to perform to customary jump upward together with the entire congregation and say: "Just as I dance in front of you yet cannot touch you, so may my foes be unable to harm me."

Now the pale crescent was hovering far above, cold and aloof. Yet there was something comforting, reassuring in the presence of this familiar face.

The snow-covered barbed-wire fences, the trees, and the barracks rooftops beckoned back with millions of brilliant starlets of their own. The birds effused the air with their night-prayer hymns. The entire universe was attired and adorned in splendid beauty like a bride before her nuptials. The angelic hosts of the bygone day uttered hymns and praises to their Creator, thanking Him for the opportunity of having served Him even for one day, and faded into oblivion. Myriads of white-winged new angels reported themselves before the Throne of Glory to take up their night vigil with choruses and melodies such as no ear has ever heard.

Yet, amidst all this splendor and sweet music, the Almighty leans backwards in His Throne of Glory, dark sadness and gloom enveloping His countenance. On this night He takes no delight in the hymns, praises, melodies, and choruses. No, He is not mourning the fall of Jerusalem and the destruction of His Holy Temple by Nebuchadnezzar or Titus. These happened many centuries ago. How long, after all, is the limit on bemoaning such remote tragedies? Now the Almighty is grieved by the affliction of His children now and here.

Down on earth, people went to movies, to concerts, embraced one another in dance, made love, quarreled, hated each other, kissed their children good night, read a letter just arrived from their son stationed in one of world's slaughterhouses, gave birth to babies, buried their dead, sipped tea in front of their fireplaces, and engaged in all the normal activities of the human race.

In Buna, surrounded by Waffen-SS, dreadful dogs, and machine-gun triggers, ten thousand frightened and emaciated slaves, shivering in the relentless cold, are waiting to be led away to "an unspecified destination."

The counting was still in process. This counting, however, was different from all other countings. On all other mornings we were counted with the knowledge that we would come back in the evening and be counted again. This time, it might well be the last counting of all. Therefore, it must be perfect, flawless. The SS, the kapos, the guards in the watchtowers, even the German shepherds, exhibited clear signs of nervousness. All this, before the Great March had even begun.

In our ranks, fatigue, despondence, and sheer weakness began to show their signs. For once, our captors had dealt us a great favor.

They had not disclosed the full extent of what was in store for us. Had we known in advance what we were to endure, that night, the day after, and the night that would follow, most of us would have chosen to be shot on the spot. Human perseverance, however, grows proportionately with the power of one's faith and tenacious hope. Only in retrospect does one look back in amazement, realizing against what overwhelming odds he wrestled and prevailed.

In the messianic age, thus the Rabbis tell us, the Holy One, blessed be He, will present Satan, tied in chains, to both the wicked and the righteous. In the eyes of the former he will seem as a tiny hill; to the latter he will resemble a tall mountain. Both will cry. The wicked will say, "See, such a small hill, and we were too weak to conquer it." The righteous will say, "Look, what a great mountain, yet we did conquer it!"

"*Achtung! Vorwärts marsch!*"

Like wild echoes from a netherworld these sudden shouts burst forth. Repeated by all the kapos and unit commanders they struck our eardrums like thunder. The great multitude had been set in motion; the March had begun.

This time the band did not play the usual music; the game was cold and brutal, no more pretending. It was for the last time that we were marching through the familiar gates—there would be no returning in the evening. No SS men were watching for a wornout shoe or a limping foot. The bandstand was deserted, orphaned. The silence, like the frost, was cutting to the very bones. Only footsteps could be heard. Thousands of feet ascended and descended monotonously, listlessly, marching into the night of the unknown.

In the beginning, one really did not have to exert himself at marching. He was carried along by sheer inertia, by the rhythm of the masses. The SS guards seemed to be pleased, even surprised, with how well everything was progressing. The snow too kept up with the rhythm—there was no letup in its descent; it kept on falling without cessation. Perhaps, when all is said and done, those gentle, soft flakes were God-sent—they kept us alert and supplied much-needed moisture for our dry tongues.

The books tell us that at an extraordinary and most unusual juncture in a person's life, visions of bygone events, long forgotten, now come and revisit him. Unlike in a dream, they present themselves as real, plastic, alive.

As I was carried along that night among thousands of captives, I saw myself a prisoner of the Chaldeans carried away in chains along the rivers of Babylon. They had just ravaged Jerusalem, burned the Temple, and wantonly killed the princes of Judea and the saints of the Most High. In a luxurious boat on the river, the victorious generals and nobles of Babylon were feasting and celebrating. One of them sighted among the captives a group of men carrying harps and flutes. He shouted to them, "Sing us some of the famous songs of Zion!" The levitical singers would not desecrate their sacred calling by entertaining the enemy, so they replied, "How can we sing the Lord's song in a foreign land?" In order to convince their tormentors of their irrevocable determination, they hung their harps on the willows in the river and mutilated their thumbs. Even if forced, they had disabled themselves from playing the instruments used in the Temple for the sacred service.

As the captives were led on their endless journey without food and water, many of them died of exhaustion, thirst, starvation. Yet the Chaldeans would not let them be buried—their carcasses became prey to the vultures and the jackals.

Then I found myself in Roman chains. Together with thousands of Judeans I was led to Rome by the victorious legionnaires of Titus. The ruins of the Temple still smoldering, the last Zealots rounded up and decapitated or crucified, I was on a ship at sea among hundreds of boys and girls on the way to Rome to be sold there into slavery and to houses of ill-fame. In the midst of a group of children there was a boy whose eyes were flaming, his golden hair overflowing like beautiful waves. He was very attractive and seemed to be a leader. Turning to the children, he said in a loud voice, in Mishnaic Hebrew, "It is written in the Psalms, 'I will bring them back from Bashan, I will bring them back from the depths of the ocean.'" The Roman centurion looked on but did not understand what the youth was saying. He only knew that all the children became agitated as the beautiful lad with the golden locks went on, saying, "By this we were promised that he who commends his soul into the hands of the Almighty by sanctifying His name, even from the depths of the ocean will he be restored before His Presence."

No sooner did the lad conclude his fiery exhortation than the children, boys and girls alike, jumped overboard and were swallowed up by the roaring waves. Unbelieving and dumbfounded the centurions looked on in dismay. A huge hand of fire descended from heaven and sank in the ocean close to the place where the children, eight hundred in all, had found their final resting place.

To my left there was marching a boy my age. I knew him from Buna; we had worked in the same kommando. He was very thin and pale, yet he kept up his pace. We neither looked at each other nor talked. It was of the utmost importance to look ahead, to walk, to march, to be part of the great mass, of the moving wave. To lose the rhythm, the inertia, could have detrimental consequences. Also, it was likewise important to be detached from oneself, from one's own marching body. To soar in one's fancy to distant heights, to remote and archaic eras and places, had the beneficial effect of blunting the pain, the fatigue, and the cold.

To my right, there was marching a man of about forty. I didn't remember whether or not I had ever met him. He seemed apathetic, resigned. From time to time I would pull his hand, even hit him, yet he hardly reacted. He uttered some names, perhaps those of his children, his wife, and other incoherent words. Then he said quite clearly in Yiddish, "I cannot anymore." He fell to the ground. The wave kept on moving; white snow kept on falling. Then a shot was heard, coming from the direction where the anonymous man had fallen. The human wave moved ahead, snow came down from above, more people fell by the wayside; more shots pierced the monotonous silence of the night. The living managed not to be hindered by the dead in their stride forward. As long as one was in command of his faculties, the supreme command was to march, to keep abreast, not to falter.

Here and there, as we passed villages and towns, we saw houses. In some of the windows there was light; from some of the chimneys smoke was ascending heavenward. It seemed unreal, unnatural, to imagine that there were people sitting in warm and well-lit homes. We passed them by, leaving them behind. The column of marchers, the road, and the snow-covered horizon were stretched out in front of us as a menacing beast. Yet by now it had become amply clear that whoever stumbled or faltered invited a bullet for himself.

Two SS guards were walking close to me; they were engaged in a conversation which I was able to overhear. Not suspecting, apparently, that someone in the crowd understood Romanian, they spoke candidly. One of the two sounded quite pessimistic. He expressed doubt whether he would ever see his family in Timisoara.

Bursts of gunfire had become a routine ingredient of our endless march. Breaking the monotony of silence, they also served as a booster to our sapped spirits; they served as an unquestionable warning and reminder, leaving everyone wondering when his turn would come.

Brightness appeared on the horizon. As if by a magic spell, darkness gave way to light. A new day was dawning on us, another day of Creation. Yet no destination was in sight. The transition from endless night into the brightness of a new day, no doubt, bolstered our spirits and our tenacity to survive.

In the distance, far off, yet quite visible, there was a huge structure standing all by itself. It was surrounded by a broad and long brick wall. Rumors quickly spread through the ranks that the structure was our destination. As soon as we reached it, we wouldn't have to march anymore. Whatever the nature of the structure, and whatever was going to happen to us when we reached it, didn't really matter. All that mattered was for the march to come to an end, to be able to rest our weary legs and bodies. Even the SS guards seemed to be more lively; they encouraged us to keep up, to make it. We did.

With great expectations and with trepidation we entered the compound. There was nothing there but a howling waste and a great emptiness. The structure inside the enclosure was a ruin without doors or windows. There was no water, no facilities, nothing. Some of the older prisoners warned us not to sit down. Yet many did not heed them. Exhausted to the last drop of their strength, they threw themselves on the first piece of available empty land that came their way. It turned out to be their ultimate resting place. Slowly, unmoved, they froze to their deaths.

Gentle, heaven-sent, brilliant snowflakes weaved pure-white shrouds around their bodies. Tiny white hills sprung up during the day throughout the enclosure, entirely changing its erstwhile landscape. Nobody lamented, nobody said the Kaddish.

For those who made it through the day, there awaited another hellish night of marching. As it later bacame obvious, our interim destination was Gleiwitz, the nearest operating railway station. The Germans made it a point to march us only at night.

29

A Remnant

AT DARK, THE living moved out again, bound for Gleiwitz, the nearest operating railway station.

I can't tell you when we arrived in Gleiwitz; I had lost all measure of time. We moved forward because we had to move forward.

My primary awareness during the second night's march was of snow falling softly upon my neck and outstretched tongue. The corpses over and around which I marched might as well have been rocks in the roadway.

I do recall vividly the absolute disorder that prevailed at Gleiwitz. The station and the adjacent camp were serving as a transit center for all the camps in the area, which were being evacuated before the advancing Soviet troops could arrive on the scene. The thousands of prisoners converging upon Gleiwitz were there regrouped for dispatch into the heartland.

As soon as my unit arrived, the SS got busy with a selection. At one spot in camp, there was a narrow passageway between two clusters of barracks.

As we moved through the passage, an SS officer looked us over. Some prisoners he directed into the barracks, others he ordered to go on. I was ordered into the barracks.

Inside, I threw myself onto one of the bunks, covered myself with a blanket, and dropped exhausted into sleep. I hadn't eaten for nearly two days, didn't imagine any food was available. Be that as it may, sleep was more critical; I couldn't have moved even if the barracks had erupted in flames.

Shots fired at close range did awaken me. Had I slept one, five, ten, or twenty-four hours?

I glanced around the barracks, horrified to find myself alone. Everyone else was outside. Looking out the window, I saw heavily armed SS men holding back a frenzied throng wanting to break out of the compound. Repeatedly, shots signaled the end of another prisoner too intent upon escape.

They were trapped; I was trapped. I went out into the yard.

Each time a prisoner was shot, two others were called to drag away the body. The carriers never returned. Before long, we recognized this task as an escape route and many rushed forward to volunteer. More deaths, more bodies, but now they were left to lie where they fell.

Having somehow found two Buna friends of my age, I hung with them, each of us feeling the crush of death.

Then, there, on the other side of the gate, stood our German Kapo. Desperately, cautiously, we signaled to him.

He approached the nearest guards. Pointing to us, he told them he had sent us into the compound to do some chore, he appealed for our release.

I could tell from their faces that the guards were well aware of the ploy, yet they let us go.

Like stones from David's sling, we flew out of the compound and toward the prisoners gathered at the other end of the camp. I expected every second to receive a bullet, but none was fired. We three had gained refuge in the midst of the other group.

The prisoners we left behind were never seen again. The rumors said they were taken into the forest and shot.

Darkness descended. Our souls darkened, and our bodies shook with cold and fright. We understood that the previous days were only a prelude to greater agonies.

Things were out of joint with the German war machine. Yet, if systems had crumbled, the commitment to the Final Solution had not. If we didn't die here, then elsewhere was seemingly our destiny.

Or, might a remnant again survive?

As best as I can remember, the last hours spent at Gleiwitz marked the first time I reflected upon my parents and brothers without wanting to, struggling to push my thoughts back to the depths of subconsciousness. Had any of my family survived? Where were they, and how did they fare?

An announcement; shrill, welcome. We were summoned to form a soup line, we were going to be fed after three days of nothing, of deadly cold.

I shall never forget that soup; it seeped into my being like milk and honey. There were no counts, no controls, no order—one could return to the line as long as the soup held out.

Then order was restored, and we were again marshaled into lines, those of us still able to move.

We marched, from compound to railroad station. The snow was falling again, its crystalline brightness almost blinding.

A long line of rolling stock awaited us; cattle cars, open to wind and snow.

Shouts and rifle butts herded us into the cars. No sooner had we been jammed inside than the engine's whistle cut the air, and the wheels began rolling.

Except for those trips to and from the yeshiva at Mihályfalva, when, of necessity, I had ridden the bus, I much preferred to journey by train. There is something imposing, something majestic about a train. Its very size and immense power, the whistle of the locomotive, the clickety-clack of the wheels fascinated me. A train never stopped for pedestrian, bicycle, car, or horse and wagon. At crossings, I liked to note the long lines of people and vehicles hoping for the train to pass.

Actually, I didn't travel much as a child and always envied the conductors, who could ride the train every day, all day or night.

Jews generally preferred to travel by train rather than by bus. Finding a quiet corner wherein to pray without being disturbed was easier in a train than in a bus. Some conductors would even avoid asking for tickets at prayer time, choosing to come back later—when they knew they would be generously rewarded for each courtesy.

I was once more entrained; there was no quiet place for prayer, barely room to stand amid my 109 fellows, even if emaciated.

Initially, the crowding had its merits; it retarded the loss of heat from our bodies if we dwelled on the inside of the car.

But even this comfort was lost in another anguish. My feet became numb; changing my position or shifting my weight was impossible.

Real hell, however, began with the onset of evening. Where there had not been even room enough to stand, we now en masse fought to sit, legs drawn up, arms and head upon knees. We shoved, we swarmed; primitive in our fury and madness.

How did we know that none of us could have lived without assuming this posture of rest? How, in fact, did we accomplish the change?

In Temple times, during the festivals, tens of thousands of pilgrims converged upon the holy city of Jerusalem. The rabbis of those generations recorded ten miracles experienced by the pilgrims. Of these, one spoke to our experience. Although the people on the Temple Mount stood closely pressed together, they found ample space to prostrate themselves at that moment when the high priest pronounced the Holy Name.

Finally, surely after hours of struggle, our roaring ocean of heads, limbs, and bodies ceased churning. Head bent upon supporting knees, eyes closed, I heard the sounds of night. Wind, dogs, the animals of field and forest, train whistles, rolling wheels, and the groans and sighs of my carmates. The symphony was strange, a cacophony befitting hell.

I escaped the horror, imagining myself on a trip to visit my paternal grandparents in the hamlet of Sinover in the Carpathian Mountains. I first visited there when I was fourteen, spending an entire winter.

Next I relived a trip from Nyirbátor to Debrecen when I was fifteen. Although the distance was not great, the train ride lasted almost the entire night. The line was local, antiquated. The gauge was broader than that on the rest of Hungary's rail system, the train slow and shaky. The night journey was excruciating, nonetheless mysterious and appealing.

When I was ten, I traveled from Mihályfalva to Nagyvárad on the eve of Shavuot to make my first visit to the Vizhnitzer Rebbe. Father, too, came to Nagyvárad to spend the festival at the rabbi's court. We lived in Szatmár, itself the seat of a famous Chassidic dynasty, but our family were adherents of the Vizhnitzer dynasty.

Inevitably, my transport from Szatmár to Auschwitz came to mind. I tried to reconstruct every minute, every sound, word, event of those three days. At first, and to my bewilderment, all I could experience was silence, nothingness.

Then I remembered something; in the Szatmár ghetto mother had handed me a pair of white socks, insisting I put them on then and there. I seldom wore white socks and saw no need for them, but she could not be dissuaded. She also had white socks ready for father and Shiele.

Had those socks been her final provision for her husband and youngest sons? For I suddenly realized, Jews dress their dead in white.

Something awful was happening, disrupting my thoughts; or were they dreams? Upon my shoulders, neck, and head, someone was settling, heavy, unmindful of my person or circumstances.

At my first awareness of this strange burden, I told myself I was mistaken, hallucinating. But then, suffocating, I tried to push the devil away. He didn't move, instead muttered something in French. I repositioned myself so that I could again breathe freely. The change worked for a short while. Then again I was suffocating. Panicked, I shoved harder this time, but again with no results. Suddenly realizing I was being too dainty, I drove my fingernails into his softer parts, quickly ridding myself of this yoke of death.

Once more cradled in the bosom of the human cargo, lulled by the rolling wheels, I returned to dreams and visions. They came faster now, in no apparent order. From time to time the train stopped, and I would force aside a small curiosity to know where, really preferring to remain semiconscious. I needed to dream, to hallucinate.

I was in a very large synagogue filled with worshippers; some of them I knew, but most were strangers. The chants I heard were not just unfamiliar, they were totally foreign, bizarre.

I wanted to join in the prayers, but they made no sense; I stood dumbfounded, unable to utter even one word. I opened a prayer book. It was unlike any other I had ever seen, and I knew all the prevailing versions of the Siddur and the Machzor, whether in the Sephardic or the Ashkenazic tradition.

I went over to the Jews whom I believed I knew and looked into their faces; they stared back as only strangers can.

If I knew none of these people, none of their prayers, what was I doing among them?

At length my rational processes came to the fore and I decided that perhaps I had come to a synagogue of the Belzer Chassidim, for I had been named after the Belzer Rebbe, who died less then seven days before I was born. Although we followed the Vizhnitzer Chassidic dynasty, father considered it a rare opportunity and privilege to have a son born within the mourning period for so great a luminary of the Chassidic world. There had been no Belzer Chassidim in Szatmár, and, as a youth, I had often toyed with the idea of sometime spending a holiday at the Belzer court.

Pain. The Frenchman was back. I wanted my dreams, told myself he was not back. But when I couldn't breathe I evicted him, this time with sophisticated, twisting pinches. He left, vindictively taking with him my Belzer court.

When the first rays of dawn penetrated our cattle car, I looked up, over the gallery of heads slumped upon knees, and there off to my left was the Frenchman, stretched atop whatever collection of souls had not yet sent him packing.

Later, in broad daylight, the train halted in the middle of a field. Snow-covered houses and barns sprinkled the horizon, the silence was acute.

Now, many were awake, standing, looking around. Wrapped in our blankets, unshaven, gaunt, we undoubtedly appeared as if just emerged from our graves, about to wander off, searching for salvation.

We were the living dead. The real dead we were ordered to throw out into the field. I shuddered; in spite of all the death I had witnessed, this disposal unnerved me.

On the second night, our struggle for space was not as fierce. But I began to experience the sores and aches suffered in the pressure and rubbing of our first night.

And again there was evening and there was morning, and the train again stopped to discharge its dead.

Not once were we given food or water. And I learned that thirst is far more difficult to bear than hunger. After three or four days of fasting, the body makes some measure of accommodation, loss of fatty tissue. But the urge for water never subsides; my tongue burned, my bowels flamed.

One day, a prisoner produced a cup, another a length of cord. The cup was lowered outside the car, dragged along in the snow, then pulled back inside. Some men were thus able to wet their tongues. For the rest of us, this divining was both diversion and hope—until the guards discovered and confiscated our water line.

Those who could, drank urine.

Once, our cortege stopped inside a railroad station. Opposite us stood a passenger train converted with beds and stretchers, transporting maimed soldiers. While they waited, ladies of mercy brought them soup and sandwiches.

Looking at them and then at us, I wanted to shout, shake the world with my anger at the madness of the human race. I was too weak even to whisper.

And on we rolled. After a week, we could stretch out full in the car, but we were colder, even with blankets obtained from the dead we had dumped. Near the end, we didn't have strength enough to throw out the bodies; they remained with us. While they were still soft, we used them as pillows and cushions for our own aching bodies. Frozen, the dead were of no comfort to us.

On the eleventh day, toward evening, we reached the end of our transport. Only twelve in our car had survived.

I saw no station, only people moving toward us. They wore prison garb.

Bodies were piled everywhere.

A gate bore the slogan *Arbeit macht frei,* "work liberates."

Our car was slung open; we were ordered out, to march toward the mountains. At first, I couldn't; I was too weak, my legs unresponsive. I was convinced, I started marching.

Our destination, less than an hour's distance, was a pass in the mountains, and within that a valley, and then another camp.

Later I learned that it was the infamous Dora, near Nordhausen.

We were taken to the showers, everyone running to the faucets to fill up with water. That was a mistake. Having been severely dehydrated, most of us now developed diarrhea.

After showers, we were taken to the infirmary and placed four in a bunk, two heads at each end. My entire body was spotted with bruises—"From the soul of the foot even unto the head there is no soundness in it, but wounds and bruises and festering sores."

Every movement, every touch was extremely painful. And there we lay, four Isaiahs in a bunk.

We received something to eat; I don't remember what it was.

All night the infirmary lights stayed on; all night orderlies walked past the bunks, looking at the sick. Whenever they decided one had died, they fastened a strap around his neck and dragged him off.

In the morning, a bunkmate was gone; the next morning, a second.

How long I recuperated is another detail I cannot remember, but at last I was released, assigned to a barracks and a labor kommando.

I was back at work, still not free.

30

Arbeit Macht Frei

COMPARED WITH DORA, Buna had been a pleasant place. Here, food was more scarce, less nourishing, working hours were longer and more demanding.

I spent three months in Dora, yet I hardly recall anything of that camp. I was truly starving, dragged through my waking hours in dizziness.

Following the first few days of work in the tunnels inside the mountain, it became clear that we were assembling huge bombs. Great numbers of German officers and civilians were involved in every detail of production; obviously, this place was superimportant.

After the war, I learned that we had been producing Hitler's V-2 rockets, used against the cities of Great Britain.

One evening when exiting the tunnel to join my unit for counting, I could see large objects suspended from the ceiling ahead of me. Coming closer, I recognized them as bodies, half a dozen people hanging like beef in a slaughterhouse.

Bits and pieces of rumor revealed that the dead prisoners were saboteurs, assembly-line workers who misassembled the rockets. If their execution had been intended as a warning, a force more powerful must have been at work, for the hangings continued, and increased.

That year, 1945, Passover was early; the weather still quite cold. On the eve of the festival, at dusk, a group of us gathered in a corner to celebrate. It seemed impossible.

How could I rejoice in a freedom granted thousands of years ago while I was yet numbered for extermination? How could we recite the opening statement of the Passover Haggadah, "This is the bread

145

of poverty our ancestors ate in the land of Egypt," when we had nothing at which to point as custom required?

I remembered how, in the wilderness, the Hebrews longed for the fish, cucumbers, melons, leeks, and garlic of Egypt; how they were blessed with quail and with manna every day. No such miracle occurred for us in Dora; all we had was poverty and bitterness.

But we did have a redeemer among us. His eyes burned like torches, his face flamed. Trembling, he began telling the miracles performed by the Almighty that His people might go free. He recounted the afflictions visited upon Pharaoh and the Egyptians, who acted contrary to the word of God. Then, in a trance, he shifted from the distant past to the glorious messianic future when those most privileged and rewarded would be the martyrs who had died sanctifying His holiness. The Lord Himself would tender a banquet for the faithful at which Leviathan would be served and wines preserved in His cellars would be poured in abundance.

That man gave us hope. He instilled purpose for our suffering and re-created the future in our hearts.

Yet the Festival of Freedom did not bring an end to our sufferings. On the contrary, our hardships increased and multiplied. Food became more and more scarce, and executions became commonplace.

Then, one day, came the inevitable order to evacuate Dora. Again we marched to the railway, were locked in cattle cars.

I recall neither the length of this transport nor its conditions. All I remember is that we arrived at a camp called Bergen-Belsen.

31

Last Days

WHILE MY ELEVEN-DAY train ride from Buna to Dora still lingers vividly in my mind—the long stops, the devastating hunger, the murderous frost, the dead bodies—I hardly remember anything of the ride from Dora to Bergen-Belsen. I must have been too weak and dazed, or just apathetic about what was going on around me.

One thing, though, I do remember. How could I not? Almost daily we had air raids; Allied planes flew over us unloading their deadly cargo. We felt strangely ambivalent in this situation. While we rejoiced on seeing the planes, none of us wanted to have his limbs or his entrails torn away by bomb or shrapnel, be it American, British, or Russian.

Casualties accompanied each raid. Whenever the planes approached, we were ordered to lie down in the car, while our SS guards ran for cover some hundred or two hundred meters away. Yet as they lay there under the shelter of a hill, an embankment, or some bushes, their machine guns were aimed in our direction. If a prisoner lifted his head out of the car, a shot would be fired in that direction. In spite of this, there were escape attempts, although I had no way of knowing how many succeeded and how many were shot.

During one raid a spectacular thing happened. The planes flew very low over us but did not drop bombs. They turned away, then came back again, circling over a radius of a few kilometers. Repeating this maneuver several times, they eventually unloaded their deadly payload—not on us, that is, but on our guards. Some of them were killed. Those who returned to the train took out their vengeance on us with beatings and curses.

In Belsen, chaos and disorder reigned supreme. There was total disintegration wherever I turned. This time, we were not turned over to anybody, just let loose to roam around aimlessly among thousands of half-dead, hollow-eyed, listless prisoners. In corners, under trees, and on stairways, there lay corpses which no one bothered to remove. Under such circumstances, everyone had to look, himself, for shelter and food.

While still in Dora I met David, a boy of my age from Hungary. We promised each other to stick together to the end and to sustain each other in whatever situation we might encounter. David, like me, had been a yeshiva student, and we shared similar backgrounds. The friendship we pledged to each other, no doubt, played a cardinal role in the survival of both of us during those last days and hours of the hell through which we'd been living.

Our first concern in Belsen was to find a corner, however small, where we could lay down our heads and tired bodies. As a result of the utter chaos and confusion, this was by no means an easy task. To our luck, and delight, we did find a room with two quite comfortable beds and plenty of blankets. The building had previously housed German officers, who had by now vacated it. Still, there was nothing to eat.

David and I went down into the street to get acquainted with the situation. We joined the multitudes who were desperately looking for food, just as we were. Here and there I saw SS officers wearing white armbands. Although I did not realize at the time that the SS men had decided to surrender, and were wearing the armbands as a precaution against being shot when the first Allied troops arrived on the scene, it was obvious from their behavior that they were no longer concerned with the prisoners and instead were preoccupied with themselves. It had not yet occurred to anyone to overpower our former tormentors, however, and in any case they were still armed with pistols.

Looking at the fences, I realized for the first time that the camp was not guarded by Germans, but by Hungarian soldiers. They too were wearing white armbands. Such novelties, however, did not overly impress me. My overriding concern at the time was food.

Like ants and carrion-seekers, thousands of skeletonlike, starving prisoners roamed the streets, picking and digging up every conceivable spot in their frantic search for food. Others, who couldn't move any more, lay swooning in their beds and in the streets until death delivered them from their agonies.

At a distance, toward the farther end of the block, I noticed a commotion and a shoving around of people. Soon, everybody was running in that direction. David and I joined the crowds, but could not get close enough to the site of action. I could see, though, that a fierce struggle was raging there; yet couldn't make any sense out of it.

When the spectacle was over and the crowds had disappeared, I saw people running in all directions, squeezing to their bosoms some round objects I could not identify. Some held one, some two, even three of the objects, pressing them to their breasts as would mothers trying to protect their babies from being snatched away by a terrible foe.

An underground cache of turnips had been discovered by someone. Soon the pit was unearthed, and the pillage began. Unfortunately for those who had arrived first, they were trampled to death by the swelling crowds.

By the time David and I arrived on the scene, there were no turnips left. On the abandoned battleground, I counted some twenty dead or half-dead people, some still writhing in the throes of beckoning death. Disappointed, David and I returned to our room, climbed into our beds, and fell asleep.

I didn't know whether I had slept an hour, a day, or two days when I was awakened by the sounds of terrible shouting and pleas for mercy. I looked out of the window and saw a disgusting sight. The street in front of my window had become the scene of a mass lynching. Some ten corpses, mutilated beyond recognition, were already lying in the street. Others were still being manhandled with fists, feet, clubs, bottles, and iron bars. The beaten men emitted pleas of mercy in German and in Polish, then fell silent.

Soon it became clear that the victims were kapos who had mistreated the prisoners in their charge. Now it was enough for one to shout "kapo" and point an accusing finger at a suspect to have him condemned to death by the other prisoners. In short, the street became one gigantic bedlam. People were dropping from exhaustion, others were being murdered in a rage, in a furious revenge. Too exhausted to care about what was going on around me, I went back to my bed and fell asleep.

Once more my sleep was disturbed, this time by roaring noises, clanging metal, and powerful engines. Still in bed, I could sense the noises coming ever closer in my direction. Even in the stupor I was experiencing, I tried telling myself that the noises were real and of the utmost significance. Yet I could not summon the energy needed to get out of bed and investigate the events. The noises were already so close that the walls of my room, even my bed, were trembling. I heard shouts of "Hurrah" coming from the mouths of great multitudes in all conceivable languages.

Someone was pulling me from bed. I resisted. It was David, who seemed determined to get me out of bed by all means. Eventually, he prevailed. Together we went down into the street.

Thousands of frenzied inmates were crying, throwing their hats into the air, and waving their hands at British soldiers who were dumbfoundedly watching the grotesque spectacle. Some of the soldiers stood mute in their tanks, tears rolling down their cheeks. The intensity of the experience was so overwhelming that I had to do something to convince myself it was real and not a delirium.

We had been liberated!

Our troubles, however, did not change in the least. The units of the British fighting forces that liberated Bergen-Belsen were not adequately equipped or large enough to handle the thousands of starving and disease-stricken former concentration camp inmates.

The first action of the British was to warn us of the dangerous consequences that might result from overeating. That certainly sounded like a bad joke. There was no such danger! In the meanwhile, people kept on dying from starvation. Later, though, the warning strikingly justified itself.

Not being able to do much for the living, the British decided to do something with the heaps of corpses strewn all over the camp. They rounded up some fifty SS personnel, charging them with the task of collecting and burying the dead. A huge pit was dug, and bulldozers shoved the dead bodies into it. The Tommies were quite strict with their SS prisoners. They used the butts of their rifles whenever the Nazis showed signs of slackness. We, the prisoners of yesterday, greatly delighted in the spectacle, although our empty stomachs kept on murmuring just the same.

Some of the former prisoners took joy in spitting at the SS men and shouting curses at them. Yet that was the limit of what the Tommies would allow us. Beatings were a privilege reserved for them only, and they utilized it quite generously.

A day or two following the liberation I felt my energies spent, my willpower sagging. I almost gave up. Then, there came a moment of grace. I was seized by panic. It suddenly dawned on me that if I wasn't going to do something drastic and right away, I would be dead before long. There was no doubt in my mind at that moment of grace that I did not want to die. I wanted very much to live. Many a time in the concentration camp I had encountered death, yet remained indifferent to it. Now I decided to cling to life by tooth and nail. Before my eyes stood the piles of corpses I had seen strewn all over the place, then shoved into the big pit. I shuddered at the thought that I, too, could soon become one of them. It would have been unforgivable folly, I said to myself, to die now that I had been liberated. I heard myself shouting, "I want to live! I want to live!"

As I was struggling with myself, an idea flashed through my mind. I ran into the room, this time to pull David out of his bed. He resisted. I begged him, shouted at him, yet he would not respond. I shook him very roughly and said to him: "David, do you remember the Hungarian soldiers at the fence?" He opened his eyes and looked at me as if from a deep coma. I shook him again and said: "Remember the Hungarian guards at the fence? Certainly you must remember them." He nodded. I gave him some water and pulled him from his bed. He wanted to go back to the respite that sleep gave him, but I wouldn't let him. I knew if I let him go back to his sleep, he would never get up again. Besides, I also knew that alone, without David, I wouldn't make it either.

I reminded David of the Hungarian guards we had seen at the fences on the day we had arrived in Belsen. "Since both of us speak Hungarian," I said to David, "maybe those soldiers would be willing to help us."

David didn't answer. He looked at me as though I were a stranger, eyes and face expressionless. I waited, all tense and agitated. Then, rising to his feet, he fell on me, embraced me, and burst into hysterical laughter. I joined him. The two of us laughed so for quite a long time, laughing and crying simultaneously. I became concerned that both of us would die from overexertion, so I willed myself to stop.

Both David and I had now become imbued with a new purpose. Both of us had made up our minds to live. Moreover, we had decided to do something that would help us implement our decision.

It was late afternoon. We started out toward the fence where we had seen the Hungarian soldiers. From a distance we could see, to our delight that they were still there. We continued walking in their direction. When the guard closest to us saw that it was our intention to walk all the way to the fence, he held out his rifle in our direction and ordered us, in German, to stop. We did stop, at the same time shouted to him in Hungarian that we would like to talk with him.

Complexion softened, tension dissipated as if by magic, the guard put his rifle down and invited us to come over to the fence. In just a few minutes we had earned each other's confidence and friendship. He was no less happy than we to have found someone to whom he could speak in his own language. Before either David or I even had a chance to tell our new friend that we were hungry, he produced a fresh-smelling loaf of bread and gave it to us. We devoured it while our benefactor watched us eat like hungry animals.

From our guard we learned that some ten days before the liberation, the Germans had handed over the task of guarding the camp to his unit. Although Belsen had by now been liberated by the British, the latter had not deemed it prudent to let go so many thousands of disease stricken, disoriented and hungry people. The Hungarians had been ordered by their new masters to stay on the job.

Since it was already evening, Yanosh, our new Hungarian friend, advised us to return to the camp and come back next morning. There was a village some five kilometers from the camp, Yanosh told us, and he would let us go there to collect some food from the German villagers. He would like us also, he casually added, to bring along some eggs and sugar for him on our return trip from the village. Yanosh seemed fully confident that we would, indeed, return.

That night I couldn't fall asleep. I kept imagining what it would be like, next morning, when the first farmer we met would let us eat as much as we desired.

Early in the morning, David and I awakened simultaneously. We walked through the quiet, deserted streets of Belsen. We walked hurriedly, and before long we arrived at the fence. Our doubts soon dissipated when we heard Yanosh greeting us from beyond the fence. Without much fanfare he lifted up a section of the fence, motioning us to crawl through the opening.

It was a chilly April morning. Standing beyond the fence, I realized that a tremendous transformation had taken hold of me. I was a free person without fences and without guards, free to go wherever I desired. I had never imagined my freedom would present itself in such a way, furtive and uneventful. I had fancied an American or British colonel or general addressing the thousands of liberated prisoners, officially notifying them that they were free. I believed that such a monumental event deserved some measure of formality, a touch of solemnity. Yet that moment when Yanosh bent down to create an opening in the fence and I crawled through it was the most eventful moment in my life.

For a while I felt strange, unfamiliar. I looked at David, he looked at me in disbelief. Then, as if by intuition, both of us threw ourselves to the ground and started rolling in the green grass, which was still saturated with morning dew. While wallowing in the wet grass we heard ourselves emitting strange, unintelligible sounds. Horses oftentimes do so after a good meal. It didn't bother us in the least that our pajamalike suits had become drenched with dew. I licked the wet blades and breathed deeply of the cool, fresh morning air.

Free or not, a gnawing sensation of hunger soon brought me back to reality. It must have been that David too experienced a similar feeling, for he turned to me and said: "Beril, let's go. The village is over there."

32

Searching

A MOST CONSUMING urge immediately following liberation was the need to search for food. An insatiable passion to eat loomed high above all other desires. This need of ours for food, however, was less than matched by the ability of our British liberators to feed us. They may not have been provided with what was needed for such a gigantic task. The fact remains that for several days following the liberation, there was no noticeable change in our situation. David and I were fortunate, though, to have established contact with the Hungarian soldier. From our first visit to the village we brought back, among other things, a skinned and cleaned rabbit, ready for cooking, an atonement offering from one of the villagers. Nor did we forget to ask for some eggs and sugar, a goodwill offering for our new friend and benefactor, so that our secret path would be kept open for future trips. One of our biggest problems upon returning to the camp was how to conceal our provisions so that we wouldn't be attacked and robbed by the starving inmates who were roaming the streets in search of food.

Our first encounter with German civilians in their home was dramatic. It was about eight o'clock in the morning. Only the lady, in her mid-thirties, her two young children, and an elderly woman were at home. David's and my sudden appearance threw them into panic and shock. We must have been the first *Musulmen* they had encountered face-to-face. They looked at us dumbfounded and speechless, examining us nervously from top to bottom, not knowing what to say or what to expect. They seemed tremendously relieved when I asked whether we could have something to eat. David and I then were served our first normal breakfast in almost a year. To us it looked more like a royal banquet. Both women showed great eagerness to serve us well and to please us, while the two children looked at us in amazement. No questions were asked and no meaningful conversation developed, as both parties, hosts and guests alike, sensed the uniqueness of the encounter.

It must have been that somehow the lady managed to summon her husband home from wherever he was. Only then did I notice that while David and I were glutting ourselves with our royal banquet, the older of the two children had disappeared. He now returned with his father, a robust farmer of about forty, quite tall, and heavily mustached. Not overly successful in trying to conceal his surprise, Herr Gerhard went out of his way to make us welcome and extend his hospitality. When David and I had finished breakfast, our host went into another room and soon returned with a small, fancy box in his hand. With a gesture of special importance he opened the box and took out of it two enormous cigars, handing one to me and one to David. Never before had I smoked either cigars or cigarettes. As I took the first inhalation of the aromatic smoke, I almost suffocated. For a long time I continued coughing and choking intermittently. Herr Gerhard hit me on my back and pressed with his hands against my chest, while the two ladies and the children looked on in terror. When I eventually relaxed and threw the cigar away with disdain, a loud laugh of relief burst forth from everyone present, and the atmosphere became less tense.

The spontaneous group relaxation surely had an easing impact on Herr Gerhard, who now produced from somewhere a pitcher full of beer and three schooners. Placing these at the center of the table, he seated himself directly across from the place where David and I were sitting. Filling up the schooners with gold-brilliant, foaming beer, our host imbibed a long sip of the liquid, leaving his schooner half-empty, then wiped his mouth with his sleeve. Looking alternately at David and at me, Herr Gerhard made it obvious that he was about to say something, but he took his time and carefully chose his words. Then, putting his right hand on his chest, he started.

"What the German people have done to the Jews is atrocious and cannot be excused. I know we shall have to pay a heavy price for it. Yet I would like you to believe me, that we, the populace, the simple people, were not aware of what was happening. We simply did not know. Please, believe me."

On that morning when I had for the first time breathed anew free air and eaten my first normal breakfast, I was not, neither physically nor emotionally, up to entering into a historical debate on the guilt or the lack of it of the German people. Nor did I possess at that time adequate and comprehensive information on what really had happened. I had not read a newspaper nor listened to a radio since my deportation from Szatmár about a year earlier. Yet I could not refrain from asking my friendly host how it was possible for him and the simple people of his village not to know what was going on within seeing distance of their homes. How could they not have been aware of the transports of thousands of prisoners arriving by train day and night? How could they be oblivious to the hundreds of dead corpses strewn all over their fields? Yet Herr Gerhard kept on insisting they knew nothing. So we left it at that. Before we departed, our host showed us a rabbit he had shot early that morning and asked us to come back later for the animal, after he had time to skin and clean it.

Some three weeks following the liberation, the first signs of life from other camps began reaching us through the lists of survivors' names that were posted at our camp office. The first published list impressed on me the frightful realities I was now to face. I knew that the search for surviving parents, brothers, and relatives would be much more traumatic and exhausting than the search for food. I also knew by then that not all the names I was searching for would ever appear on the lists. With trepidation and anxiety I stood in a long line of people with somber looks, who, like me, had come to search for the names of survivors on a list that carried a message of life, yet also implied death. From time to time, shouts of joy burst forth from the mouth of one who had just read the familiar name of one of his relatives. Many, however, left sullen and dejected.

When my turn came, I read the names over once, and then again, but found none of the names for which I was searching. In three days, a new list arrived in the camp and was posted for public view. Again, I found none of the names of my family. When the third list was posted and I read it, my blood rose to my head, and my heart pounded heavily. I saw the name Frida Herskovitz.

Frida was my first cousin; our mothers had been sisters. She too had been taken to Auschwitz from the Szatmár ghetto. According to the list, she was now at a place called Salzwedel. Without further delay, I decided to go and find her.

The best transportation system operating in Germany at that time was hitchhiking. A German truck driver took me halfway and dropped me off in some city near the office of the British military commandant. When I told the officers that I had just found the first, and perhaps the only, survivor of my family, they seemed moved and eager to help. Before anything else, however, the commandant ordered the attendant sergeant to serve me a meal. While I ate, the officers discussed various options of transportation to Salzwedel. When I finished, the sergeant gave me two packs of English cigarettes and five bars of chocolate, all of which I promptly put into my pockets for future bartering.

While I was eating, I noticed in the room a man wearing a uniform unlike the British military uniforms, which I had already learned to recognize by that time. I identified this person by the shiny metal letters attached to his lapel that read U.S. Army. It was the first time I had seen an American. Since we were in the British Zone, I assumed that the American was there on some official business. When the U.S. captain learned about my case, he came over to me, introduced himself, and told me that he was on his way to Salzwedel but had stopped at this place for some routine business, and that he would be glad to take me along in a short while. The fine meal I had been served, the chocolate and the cigarettes, and now the good news I heard from the American captain made my day.

Hardly was I seated in the U.S. Army jeep when I thought I was flying in a helicopter. In order not to be thrown out of the jeep, I had to hold fast to my seat with both of my hands. Following a ride of approximately two hours, I saw a sign that read "Salzwedel."

While I was hitchhiking, and while I was riding in the American jeep, a gnawing doubt disturbed my peace of mind. The list that contained the name Frida Herskovitz did not give any additional information about her, except the fact that she was at Salzwedel. It could be that she was not my cousin but another person with the same name. The captain, to whom I revealed my doubts, tried to assure me that it was, indeed, my cousin. He also promised not to just drop me off at camp, but to stay with me until I found Frida.

We arrived at a place that had long rows of nice-looking brick buildings, many trees, green lawns, and many flower beds. Well-dressed girls in their upper teens and young ladies were strolling among the blooming trees or resting on the well-tended lawns. Pleasant sounds of music coming from various directions permeated the afternoon air, creating a sensation of nostalgia and peacefulness. Later I learned that the place had previously served as a vacation resort for the German military and their families, but had been converted by the British into a temporary home for some two thousand former female prisoners, mostly Jewish, who had been liberated by the British in various concentration camps in the area. By the time I came to Salzwedel, there were also some fifty men at the camp. Like me, they had come there to search for surviving family members.

The U.S. captain kept his promise. He took me to the camp office and did not leave until I had, indeed, found my cousin. Both he and his driver watched the emotional reunion of two survivors, and both he and his driver turned aside for a moment to wipe away a tear, so as not to betray a momentary sentimental weakness unbecoming two hardened military men.

Ever since, the suspicion has not escaped me that the U.S. Army captain really had no business to attend to at Salzwedel. His only reason for driving all the way there, I suspect, was to bring about a reunion between two survivors, "charred sticks plucked from the fire."

It is difficult to describe the regal treatment I was accorded by Frida and her seven roommates. Each of the eight girls tried to outdo the other in showering attention and affection on me. It was the first time since my deportation that I was sitting with my own people in a relaxed atmosphere with no fear or anxiety.

Life in Salzwedel was a veritable vacation. We, the campers, had to do nothing at all, but were given everything necessary to satisfy our needs. German civilians from the vicinity worked in the kitchens, in the dining halls, and even cleaned our rooms. Everyone was certainly free to leave the compound and go wherever he wished, yet very few left. The future was so uncertain that no one really knew what to anticipate or what course to take. The British were generous in giving us the best of everything—clothing, food, even entertainment. Many girls willingly accepted offers by British soldiers to teach them English, and they learned the new language most eagerly. During the evenings there were parties, music, and dances. The survivors enjoyed themselves. Still, maybe it was a final desperate attempt to avoid the inevitable blow of coming face-to-face with the brutal realities. No one, as yet, knew the full depth of the tragedy, and no one was eager to hasten the day when the naked truth would slap him or her in the face. The good life at Salzwedel might have continued for a long time, but it was drastically interrupted by changing circumstances.

One day, British soldiers drove through camp and announced from loudspeakers that as a consequence of territorial adjustments between the British and the Russians, Salzwedel would be evacuated by the former and handed over to the latter. The announcer added that all who wished to go along with the British should register at the camp office. The British promised to maintain at the new location the same services they had been providing us with at Salzwedel.

A heated campaign engulfed our camp as pro-British and pro-Soviet agitators roamed the streets trying to convince the inhabitants to leave with the former or to stay and wait for the arrival of the latter. Psychologically, the majority of the survivors were already conditioned to favor the Russians. While still in Hungary, we had hoped and prayed for the Russian forces to arrive and liberate us from the Nazi death grip. In their desperation, the Hungarian Jews had conceived of the Russians as redeemers and saviors who were late in coming. Now that they were at last coming to us here in Salzwedel, the excitement was great. To be sure, the British were nice guys, polite, and compassionate. One could hardly encounter a British soldier without being offered chewing gum, a cigarette, or a piece of chocolate. Yet there was nothing exciting about them. The Russians, on the other hand, had a mysterious aura surrounding them; they were still the great unknown.

By the time the deadline for registration was over, only fifty people had registered. Yet the British would not accept that as the final verdict. When evacuation hour arrived, fifty lorries pulled into the camp, their loudspeakers announcing that it was still possible to join the evacuating forces even if one had not signed up. This last-ditch attempt of the British to convince the stubborn Jewish girls to go with them ended in humiliating failure. No one took seriously the British admonition that as soon as they left, even crying would not help those who stayed behind. Typical British gentlemanliness and the comradeship forged on the battlefield prevented the British from openly saying anything nasty about their Russian comrades at arms. Yet it did not prevent them from uttering veiled hints about the type of behavior to be expected of Russian soldiers. Nothing, however, prevailed on those who had their minds already firmly made up. The lorries returned empty. It took us only one hour to find out how prophetic the British had been when they spoke of crying.

As we watched the British contingent depart in one direction, we saw in the distance, in the opposite direction, a huge moving mass—the Russians were coming. Loud applause rose from our midst. Yet something puzzled us; the Russians were moving very slowly. Why did it take them such a long time to reach us when we could already see them? Gradually the picture became clear. The Russian units assigned to take over Salzwedel were not mechanized. They rode neither tanks nor troop carriers, not even jeeps. They arrived in horsedrawn carts. The soldiers were unkempt, unshaven, and smoked vile-smelling cigarettes they themselves had made out of newsprint and cheap tobacco they called *machorka*. There was a crying contrast between the polished and refined British soldiers who had just left and their Russian replacements, who looked to us as though they had come out of the pages of a medieval-history book. Our bewilderment and disappointment were great. We looked in the opposite direction, but our British friends had already disappeared from sight. Still worse things were in store for us.

In the eyes of our new masters we were enemies, collaborators with the Germans. How otherwise could we explain the enviable living conditions we were enjoying? Besides, what were we doing in Germany in the first place if we had not come there to help the Germans in their war effort? All our explanations and pleas that we had been concentration camp inmates, and that our dear ones had been gassed, fell on deaf ears. They simply refused to believe us. Already, the girls were having a tough time warding off the insulting advances of the Russian soldiers. There was, indeed, much bitter crying, perhaps more than the British had foreseen. Still, the worst was yet to come.

A few days following their arrival, the Russian authorities told us that they needed the Salzwedel compound for their own personnel and we would have to evacuate it. They did not tell us, however, where they would take us. As we later learned, they themselves did not know what to do with us.

A day or two later, we were placed under military surveillance. Again we had become prisoners. This time we were prisoners of the Russians. We remained confined to the compound, our freedom of movement suspended. Soon after, a long convoy of military trucks moved into the camp and we all were ordered into the trucks. Unlike the British, the Russians did not ask anyone whether he wished to stay or to go; they simply gave orders. We rode off in search of a new place. Our convoy stopped at several refugee camps, but all refused to take us in, as they were already overcrowded. Once, in the middle of the night, we stopped at a camp that housed Ukrainians who had collaborated with the Germans, and who were now awaiting their forced shipment back to Russia. Horror overtook us as we contemplated the possibility of being placed together with those Nazi criminals and then being shipped to Russia as collaborators. To our delight, there too we were refused for reasons of overcrowdedness. The ride in search of a place resumed. The next day, our Russian masters simply dumped us at a huge field where the only building was a large stable. They left us in the charge of a unit of Tito's partisans who had their camp nearby. The Russians ordered the partisans to guard us and supply us with food.

There were heartrending scenes: girls wept in hysteria, bemoaning the terrible mistake we had committed by ignoring the British pleas to go with them. Yet, as the British had told us, crying made no difference in our desperate situation. Fortunately, the partisans were sympathetic and friendly, trying to alleviate our plight as much as was possible.

One afternoon, as we were cooking supper in the open field, a high-ranking Russian officer and his aide entered our compound. Of short stature and dark skin, the officer engaged in a friendly conversation with us. He inquired who we were and how we had ended up in that place. When he heard our story, he tried to remain calm, but I remember that he turned all tense and his voice became slightly tremulous. Following several minutes of tense silence, the short, dark skinned officer pointed in a certain direction and said resolutely, "Do you see those nice little brick houses over there, uphill? Well, tonight you all will be sleeping in those houses."

We stood in silent awe, not knowing what to say, nor how to take his words. Was it a cruel joke he was playing on us, or did he have some evil design on us? Before long, however, we realized he meant every word he had said, and that he intended to live up to his words. The Germans who had been living in the houses the officer had pointed at were given two hours to evacuate them. Then, we moved in. The homes were nicely furnished, and their pantries were well stocked with a variety of foodstuffs. The partisans still looked after our needs, except that they did not guard us any more. We were free people again.

Later we walked to the nearest town and in the street were identified as survivors by some local Jews. When we told them our story and of our encounter with the mysterious, high-ranking, dark-skinned Russian officer, they told us that they knew him well and suspected he was Jewish, although he had never told them so.

In a few more days, a representative of the newly established Czechoslovak government came to see us. He told us that everyone who wanted to return to Czechoslovakia should register with him. Most of the girls had been deported by the Hungarians from areas ceded to them by Hitler's edict. Those territories had by now been returned to Czechoslovakia and to Romania. Since it was unlikely that a Romanian representative would ever come to that place, I too registered with the Czech official. In a few days we were in Prague.

Among my most favorite childhood stories were those about the Golem of Prague, who was created by Rabbi Judah Loeb, the Ma-haral, in the sixteenth century. I was never satiated with the enchanting tales of that mystical creature who was always available whenever needed, and who brought salvation for Israel at the most critical times. I followed him excitedly over mountains and vales in his search for the real murderers of a Christian child whose death had been blamed on the Jewish community on the basis of the absurd libel that Jews needed Christian blood for their Passover matzot. This heinous blood-libel, which prevailed throughout Europe for close to a millennium, marred the spirit of the most joyous of the Jewish festivals, and often resulted in brutal attacks against Jewish citizens and in the destruction of their property. The Golem had been created with the express purpose of combating this evil by discovering the perpetrators of the crime and exposing their vicious designs. Whenever I read or was told these stories, I could fancy the cries of the frenzied mobs roaming the ghetto, shouting death slogans against the Jews. I saw the tortured and agitated faces of the victims, bowed under their heavy burden, terrorized, and exposed to hatred and abuse. Then, as if transported there by a whirlwind, the towering figure of the Golem appeared in the courtroom, overwhelming the attention of everyone—victim, torturer, judge, false witness, and mob. The investigation was short. Under the overpowering impact of the Golem, the real murderers confessed their crime, and for the Jews there was salvation.

Often I had wondered why the rabbis of our time couldn't get together and create their own Golem. Imagine how much suffering such a Golem could have alleviated, how many injustices he would have rectified. Whenever I was taunted or attacked, the image of the

Golem came to my mind, and I was sorry we did not have one like him. Now that I was in Prague, I made up my mind to go and see the Golem, or, rather, whatever was still left of him.

Prior to the festival of Passover of the year 1580, so the story goes, the Maharal, chief rabbi of Prague, experienced a nocturnal divine revelation. In it he was given detailed instructions on how to create a being out of earth, and instill in it supernatural powers. Early in the morning, he proceeded with two of his most able and trusted disciples to the bank of the river, where, in a muddy spot, he drew with a cane the figure of a human being about six feet tall. Following instructions in the manner of Jewish mystics, the disciples and the Maharal circled around the figure seven times, all the while uttering various combinations of the Divine Name. Gradually, the figure assumed human form with skin, hair, nose, mouth, eyes, and all of the other limbs. Finally, the Maharal cited the crucial verse from Genesis, "The Lord God formed man from the dust of the earth, and He blew into his nostrils the breath of life, and man became a living being." Ordered to rise to his feet, the Golem obeyed. The Maharal then charged his new creation to be willing to go through fire and water, and to climb mountains in the service of the Jewish people. He also promised him that neither sword, nor fire or water would have power over him.

Not knowing the language of the country, and because the Czechs adamantly refused to respond to anyone in German, it was quite difficult for me to find the Altneuschul, the ancient synagogue in the attic of which the remains of the Golem had reputedly been preserved. I wondered whether I would be able to see the secret combination of the sacred seventy-two-letter Name of the Almighty inscribed on a piece of parchment and placed beneath the Golem's tongue. It was that Holy Name, according to the stories I had been told, that endowed the Golem with his superhuman powers. Yet whenever his creator, the Maharal, suspected that the Golem was inclined to usurp too much power, and that he might get out of control and become a menace, he would order him to the ground and pull out the Holy Name from beneath his tongue. Without the Holy Name, the Golem would lie there just like a clod of earth. As the enemies of Israel lifted their heads again, and troubled times returned to plague the house of Israel, the Golem would be called upon once more to fulfill his mission.

Although I left my lodging place early in the morning, it was close to noon by the time I found myself facing the legendary synagogue. To my utter disappointment, however, the building was locked and there was no one around whom I might have asked for information. I circled the building many times, trying all the while to picture in my mind how the place had looked three of four hundred years before on an ordinary Shabbat day, on a Passover, or on Rosh Hashanah, when children were playing in the courtyard and in the adjacent streets, and the interior was packed with worshippers, many of them my age. I wondered how I would have felt had I lived in those days and prayed here in this synagogue. I tried to picture in my mind the many scholars of the Talmud and of other books of piety who gathered in this synagogue centuries ago, early in the morning and late at night, to perpetuate the word of God and to instill meaning into their lives. I thought of the thousands of young Jewish children of Prague who for centuries filled those streets with their innocent voices and pure melodies, excitedly chanting their first verses from Chumash and Rashi. The painful realities of the present, the deep silence, and the total absence of even one Jew in that venerable place made me very sad. I felt a burning desire to talk to someone, to pour out my emotions. There was no one who would listen. I decided to leave and to come back next morning much earlier.

The next day I woke up early and started for the Golem's abode. Now that I knew the way from yesterday's experience, I hoped to arrive at the synagogue in time for the morning service, when it should certainly be open. Again, even at this early hour, the building was closed, and a deep silence, a disturbing silence, hovered above the place. In a final desperate attempt, not wanting to leave the site without having seen the Golem, I searched for the secret or hidden entrance that such old buildings are reputed to have. I found none.

A lady from a nearby house, seeing my predicament, came over and asked me whether there was anything she could help me with. I told her I wanted to see the synagogue from the inside, but I did not tell her anything about the Golem. Having learned that I was a survivor of the concentration camps, the lady took pity on me, inviting me into her home, where she served me a meal. It was already too late for breakfast, and the time for lunch had not yet arrived. However, the lady did not call the meal she was serving me by any specific name, and I did not care at that time about such trivialities.

The lady was young and quite attractive, and besides a very large

German Shepherd there was no one else in the house. On the wall near the grand piano there was a picture of a uniformed handsome man and other works of art as well. Everything in the house, including the furniture, indicated that whoever was living in it was well-to-do. Several times I intended to ask the young lady about the uniformed man in the picture, but somehow I never got around to asking her. Concerning the synagogue she told me that it had been deserted ever since the deportation of the Jews of Prague. Recently, though, she had seen an elderly man who came by himself with a key in his hand, opened the building, entered it, and spent some time there, then left. She had seen the same person at least two more times, but it had been some three weeks now since she had last seen him.

All the time I was conversing with the woman, I apprehensively watched every movement of the German Shepherd, fearful lest he jump on me and devour me. Never before had I seen such a huge dog. What made me even more uneasy was the animal's having situated itself right in front of me and watching every movement of mine.

I thanked the lady for her generosity, indicating my intention to leave, yet she took no cognizance of it and continued the conversation, all the time putting more fruits and pastry on the table. The content of our conversation was rather frivolous and of no special significance. For some inexplicable reason both of us avoided the great issues of the time, nor did we talk about ourselves. Even after some two hours of such conversation we remained almost total strangers.

When I eventually got up and indicated that I was determined to leave, the woman asked me to come back in the evening. Somewhat surprised, I asked whether she thought the synagogue would be open in the evening. After a lengthy silence she said that she didn't know, but wouldn't it be good anyway for the two of us to have dinner together? Again I wanted to ask her about the uniformed man whose picture was hanging on the wall in front of the grand piano, yet I thought it inappropriate and an intrusion on her privacy. I thanked her warmly for the invitation but declined to accept it with regrets. I returned to my lodging place, where I found my friends, who told me that they had been concerned by my lengthy absence.

In a day or two I learned that although the original Jewish community of Prague had been almost entirely annihilated during the war, there was a new nucleus of a Jewish community in the capital city comprised of survivors who came to Prague from various parts of the country. Most of them had served in the notorious forced-labor brigades and had been liberated by the Russians. Several meetings with those survivors and some follow-up investigation resulted in the joyous news that two of my brothers, Hershil and Yosil, had survived, and that Hershil was in a hospital in Budapest. Without wasting any more time, I headed for Budapest.

After I arrived there, I began searching for the hospital in which my brother was confined. When I located it, I readied myself for my first meeting with a survivor of my immediate family. Not having been told anything about his condition, nor the reason for his being hospitalized, I had serious misgivings and prepared myself for the worst.

The hospital was crowded, even its corridors filled with beds. The sharp odors of medications present everywhere impressed on me my own hospital experience at Buna. Before I was led to my brother's room, a nurse was dispatched to prepare him for the visit. For some reason, whether a shortage of electricity or overcrowding, the visitors' elevators were not operating, and I had to climb to one of the upper floors on foot. All along the way on the various floors I saw maimed people, one missing a hand or a leg, one missing an eye or otherwise severely injured. These sights in no way bolstered my already flagging spirit.

As I entered Hershil's room, I saw him lying on a tall bed, slightly slanted toward his feet. His left leg was elevated and attached to a system of rails and chains from which a set of weights was suspended. A faint smile appeared on his face as he saw me entering. The stark realities of the hospital coupled with the impact of reunion under the given circumstances caused me sudden dizziness. I saw a chair nearby and sat down quickly. As I looked at Hershil, I felt somewhat reassured. His situation, after all, seemed not to be too bad, I reasoned with myself, since his head, eyes, and both hands were intact and functioning well.

It was Hershil who broke the silence, asking me whether I knew anything of Shiele or of Antshil. When I replied in the negative, his pale face trembled, and a fleeting spasm appeared at the left corner of his mouth. He did not ask about our parents. Instead, he told me that Yosil was home, and that he came quite frequently to Budapest. After a somewhat lengthy pause, and without waiting for me to ask about his leg, Hershil began telling his story.

From the day the Germans invaded Hungary, hiding in Budapest under an assumed identity had become ever more difficult. In the course of less than six months, Hershil was forced to change his identity three times. In addition, he succeeded in obtaining a Swedish *schutzpass*, which bestowed a certain degree of protection on its bearer. Yet, despite all of his papers, he was always fearful that he might be arrested as a suspect and interrogated. There was in Budapest a Jewish woman and her four children who had escaped from Poland. They posed in Hungary as Catholics, scrupulously observing the church's tenets, including regular church attendance. Originally, the children had an Orthodox Jewish upbringing. While in flight from their persecutors, they too had to change their identity several times. One Sunday in the church, when the eight-year-old boy's turn came to be given the holy wafer by the priest, the youngster asked the latter for a yarmulke. The poor, confused soul could not conceive of eating the holy bread without his head being covered.

Not only was it difficult at the critical moment for one to remember his identity, it was no less frustrating trying to follow the tilting political realities in Hungary.

On October 15, 1944, the remnant of Hungary's Jewry in Budapest rejoiced, hailing Miklós Horthy as their redeemer, for on that day the Hungarian regent proclaimed the extrication of Hungary from the Axis alliance. Since Horthy had already stopped the deportation of Jews from the country, the Jews of Budapest believed that he had also extricated them from the death grip of the Nazis. Their jubilation, however, was short-lived. It did not last for even one full day.

On the same day, the most rabid of Hungary's Jew-haters and the most avowed of Hungary's Nazis staged a coup, and, with the help of the Germans, took power in Budapest. Ferenc Szálasi, head of the infamous Arrow Cross Party, became the country's new prime minister. If up to now life in Budapest had been hell, it now became a real inferno. Sensing the dramatic changes, Eichmann returned to Budapest and feverishly threw himself into the business of liquidating the final remnants of Hungarian Jewry, now concentrated mainly in Budapest.

By that time, any semblance of law and order in the capital had completely broken down, and anarchy and terror reigned supreme. The new government almost daily issued new and often contradictory decrees concerning the Jews. Although Hungary was faced with one of the grimmest moments in her history, and the nation's most existential interests were at stake, the government was consumed with one overriding issue—the Jewish question. The Russian armies were already making deep inroads into the country, and German resistance was collapsing all along the front, yet the Hungarian leaders were able to conceive of only one menace—the Jews. The ferocious hatred manifested toward the Jews of Budapest during those final days of the war can only be categorized in terms of insanity and madness.

Rampaging bandits of the Arrow Cross took the law into their own hands, looting, shooting, and murdering any Jew whose ill fortune brought him into their reach. They also broke their way into Jewish homes, harassing and killing young and old. At two hospitals they murdered all the Jewish patients, and the Jewish doctors and nurses. A favorite pastime of the gangs was to drag their victims to the banks of the Danube River before shooting them, so that the victims' bodies would automatically fall into the water. In the city proper, thousands of Jewish bodies were piling up in hospitals and synagogues awaiting burial.

All that time, Hershil was living with a Jewish family at Teleki Tér. One night he was awakened by shouts, "They are coming, they are at the gates!" All knew who "they" were. It was enough to send anyone running for his life. Hershil, who always had a proclivity for original thought, considered it unwise to run into the street, directly into the hands of the Arrow Cross death squads. Instead, he tied a rope to a window facing a shaft, and lowered himself down from the second floor. To his misfortune, the rope broke before he even reached halfway, sending him to his destination much faster than he had planned. Immediately following his fall, Hershil felt a sharp pain in his left thigh, which he attributed to the blow he had just sustained. In order not to be discovered by his pursuers should they search the shaft, and also because the barren cement floor was quite cold, he decided to hide in an old laundry basket someone had thrown long ago into the shaft. Only then did he realize that he could not stand up on his feet. Through a strenuous effort, however, he crawled into the basket and waited for further developments.

Soon the noises quieted down and everything seemed to have returned to normal—everything, that is, except my brother's thigh, which hurt more and more. He shouted for help, and neighbors came and pulled him out of the basket and then out of the shaft. As it turned out, no Arrow Cross gangs had been active in the vicinity that night. The entire confusion was the result of someone's strained nerves, which brought about everybody's running, which in turn caused Hershil to tie a rope to his window, which broke while he was lowering himself, which resulted for my brother in a broken left thighbone.

The bandits, however, did come the next day.

In the streets of Budapest there was utter chaos, and death loomed everywhere. One never knew whether he was going to be hit by a bullet fired by a member of an Arrow Cross gang, a German tank, or a low-flying Russian airplane. While the Russian bullets were nondiscriminatory, the former two aimed their weapons mainly at Jews.

Hershil was lying in bed with a high fever and in acute pain when he heard shouts, "All Jews immediately to present themselves in the courtyard. Anyone found inside the building will be shot." All the Jewish residents began running in panic down the stairway and toward the courtyard, some of them carrying my brother with them. When, however, he shouted terribly on account of his pain, they put him down in the corridor and left him there, running for their lives. Hershil heard shots being fired all around, and fearful for his life if found by the gangs inside the building, he started crawling down the stairs on his hands and knees. An Arrow Cross gangster, however, seized him and dragged him to the sidewalk. In the street, bullets were flying in all directions, everyone shooting at everyone. Seeing him wounded and lying on the sidewalk, one of the Nazis pulled his pistol. Aiming it at Hershil he shouted wildly, "You perfidious Jew, you were wounded while shooting at our forces." "No," Hershil replied, "please, don't shoot. I was wounded in the Hungarian Labor Service, where a heavy load fell on my left leg. Besides," Hershil continued, "I am a bearer of a Swedish *schutzpass*, and the head of the Swedish legation in Budapest is personally concerned with my well-being."

The gangster put his pistol away, called over a coachman, and ordered him to "drive this Jew to the designated place." The two of them tied my brother's hands and fixed a rag over his eyes. Following an arduous ride that even more aggravated my brother's pain, he was driven into a large enclosure that had been used for cattle auctions and was dumped on the wet ground. There he joined thousands of other Jews who had been brought there during the past several days. All of them spent that night in the open, in a drizzling rain that soaked them to their bones.

The next day, the Szálasi government issued yet another of its contradictory orders, now calling for the return of all arrested Jews to their homes. Hershil and the other wounded and sick were taken to a hospital. They remained there until the liberation of Budapest by the Russian army. During that period, a Swedish diplomat, Raoul Wallenberg, paid several visits to the hospital, which was enjoying the protection of the Swedish flag.

It goes without saying that in those chaotic times and unusual circumstances my brother's leg was never given a thorough checkup. It was enough that the hospital provided him with a haven from the ravages of the streets and a certain measure of safety. Several months after the liberation, still limping on his left side, he returned to the hospital, where he underwent complicated surgery during which his left thighbone had to be broken again and properly reset. The weights I saw suspended from his left leg when I entered his room were arranged so as to pull apart the two sections of the bone that had grown together the wrong way.

The story left my brother exhausted. He was now much more pale than when I had entered his room some hours earlier. I tried to encourage him to take a nap, promising I would be back next morning. Still, he asked me to stay a little longer. I sat at his bedside until he fell asleep, then left quietly.

Jewish relief organizations, like the American Joint Distribution Committee, were already active in Budapest in extending help to survivors. I was given a small amount of cash and allocated a place where I could have room and board. My future course, however, was entirely blurred. I had a great desire to go to Szatmár, my hometown, yet I was also apprehensive about the idea of returning there. My brother's confinement in the hospital temporarily aided my decision to stay in Budapest and extend him moral support. Yet, following some two weeks of aimlessness and heightened anxiety, I made the decision to continue to Szatmár and see for myself.

33

Closing the Circle

WITH A HEAVY heart I went to take leave of Hershil. My visits with him in the hospital had become a vital part of my daily routine. In fact, I eagerly looked forward to each of our meetings. They presented the first opportunity in years for both of us to sit and talk at leisure, openly, and without regard for time. Hershil had always been a master conversationalist, possessing an innate sense of humor. He was loaded with jokes, some of which made me explode with laughter. I could easily sense that my lengthy visits with him had a positive effect on his sagging spirits. Now that I had come to take my leave of him, I could see an air of sadness overtaking him, although he tried to conceal it from me. I promised that it wouldn't be long before I was back in Budapest. Thus we parted.

In the summer of 1945, railway transportation in Hungary was precarious and irregular. Many of the locomotives, passenger cars, and freight cars had been damaged in the war. Many others had been abandoned deep in Russia, where they had transported Hungarian troops, Jewish forced-labor battalions, and supplies. Moreover, the Russian occupation forces had requisitioned much of the remaining operational rolling stock for their own needs. As a result, the few trains available for civilian travel were usually so jammed with passengers, even before they entered a station, that it was often necessary to wait for hours before one could get on a train. Travel by rail had yet another serious drawback in those days. From time to time—no one ever knew when to expect it—Russian soldiers would board the train and plunder the passengers of their watches, attractive briefcases, valises, and other valuables. They even used to steal the shoes or boots off one's feet. Women were particularly terrified. Since I possessed no valuables, I was not troubled about this aspect of the trip.

I finally managed to board a train and then had to wait impatiently for more than two hours while it sat in the Budapest railway station without moving. At long last the locomotive emitted a cloud of steam and a shrill whistle. This was soon followed by the familiar clickety-clack of the heavy metal wheels as they rolled along the glistening steel tracks. We were heading eastward.

All the way along our journey, I saw long freight trains guarded by Russian soldiers heading eastward. Quite frequently our train was held back to yield the right of way to them. They were carrying heavy machinery, grain, livestock, and a great variety of other commodities, all being taken out of Hungary and shipped to the Soviet Union as war reparations imposed on a defeated nation for having sided with Hitler.

As we passed through towns and cities, I became even more cognizant of the heavy damage the country had sustained during the war. I saw railway stations, bridges, and large buildings that were entirely or partially destroyed. Some of the bridges our train crossed were makeshift, and the crossing had to be done slowly. Yet there was also a brighter side to the scenery I observed. The famous Hungarian orchards had yielded bounteous crops in that postwar summer. All along the way, I saw in the fields men, women, and children picking luscious apples, plums, pears, and peaches from heavily laden trees. It was obvious that they were going about their work with animation, as if eager to produce enough for both conqueror and conquered.

Inside the train, few of the passengers spoke, and then only in halting voices. There were new realities to reckon with, and new circumstances. Some were not eager to talk about the past while facing an uncertain future. One had only to be denounced as a collaborator of the Nazis and he could face a denazification court. Communism, a new totalitarian ideology, had now replaced Nazism.

There was still another good reason for the depressed mood of the Hungarians. The end of war brought home some bitter realities to every Hungarian family. Not only had they lost the war; they had also suffered hundreds of thousands of casualties, and much of the national infrastructure had been destroyed. If all that was not enough, the Russians were now dismantling and carrying away the nation's largest factories. The deepest and most humiliating wound, however, and one the Hungarians would have to suffer permanently, was the loss of large territories claimed and taken away by Romania,

Yugoslavia, Czechoslovakia, and Russia. Hungary again became a truncated nation with borders similar to those imposed on her following World War I.

"Next stop Szatmár," a voice casually announced. I gave a start. Would there be anyone waiting for me? I certainly knew that the answer was no. Who could there be? I bent out through the window and observed the familiar surroundings. There, beyond the rails, in simple shacks, I sighted Szatmár's first people. It was a hot August afternoon. Playing children interrupted their activities for a moment to wave at the passing train. They were elated when the locomotive responded with a shrill whistle, then went back to their games. Those children and their families had stayed in Szatmár during the war. They had not been deported, for they were not Jewish. They looked as happy and as jovial as playing children always do. Instinctively, I thought of Shiele. Would he come back? Was it possible that at this very time he too was heading home toward Szatmár in another train? Or was he now traveling throughout Germany, visiting D.P. camps, searching for me?

The locomotive emitted a shrill whistle and lots of steam. The wheels slowed down their clicking motion and came to a halt. There was a large sign facing me which read "Satu-Mare." When I left the city, a little more than a year before, it was part of Hungary; now it belonged to Romania. I was looking for the familiar station building, but there was none. All I saw was a heap of rubble. In the war, the Russians had bombed Szatmár, and the railway station was one of their targets. It was a direct hit. I remembered better days this station and I had seen.

One morning at public school, when I was about nine years old, the teacher told the class that all of us should come next day dressed up in our best clothes. Our entire school, the teacher said, was going to the railway station to see the king. Excitement among the children rose high. In Romania, the king was held in high esteem. Every morning before classes we sang the national hymn and prayed that the king would be victorious in battle. His likeness hung in front of us constantly. Now we would be able to see him in the flesh. He would look at us and wave to us. I, too, was excited by the news. I have always been fascinated by royalty and regalia. Learning in cheder about the military groupings of the twelve tribes and their ensigns, I was disappointed that the colors of the various flags have not been specified. I knew that the flag of Judah had a lion embroidered on it; yet I wondered what its colors were. Thrice daily I prayed, "Cause the dynasty of David soon to flourish, and may it be exalted through Thy saving power." Yet this did not diminish in the slightest my patriotic loyalty to king Carol of Romania. I awaited with excitement the moment I would be able to gaze at my king's face.

Early in the morning, thousands flocked to the railway station; all the streets were scrubbed clean and decorated with the national flag. Schoolchildren marched by singing and calling out patriotic slogans. The station was hardly recognizable due to the hundreds of flags and portraits of the king. Bands played music, and the various delegates anxiously awaited their turn. A patriarchal figure with a broad-brimmed black hat and a silk-white beard was now approaching the king at the head of his delegation. Rabbi Yoilsh Teitelbaum, the Szatmárer Rebbe, took the king's outstretched hand, bowed slightly, and pronounced the traditional blessing for such an occasion: "Blessed art thou, Lord our God, King of the Universe, who hast given of thy glory to mortal man."

In later years, the Jews of Szatmár used to reminisce about that royal visit to our town. They used to say that King Carol was deeply moved by his encounter with the Szatmárer Rebbe and accorded him a measure of deference such as he did not to the heads of any of the other delegations that came to the railway station to greet him on his brief stopover.

The passengers who disembarked in Szatmár soon left for their respective destinations. I remained standing, looking around. I don't know how long I stood there in agitation and in confusion. Then I pulled myself together and walked outside the station. At first I contemplated hiring a horse-and-buggy to ride with into the city. Then I contemplated something else. I decided to relive my own Via Dolorosa of one year before. My personal belongings now no heavier than a year ago—a rucksack with only a few essentials—I thought it should not be too strenuous for me to walk all the way into the city on foot.

I walked all alone, occasionally carrying my load in my right hand, and occasionally in the left. I was following the same path I had walked a year before in the opposite direction, the same alleys, the same backstreets. Now, nobody paid any attention to me. My walking, rucksack in my hand or on my shoulder, had no meaning to those who passed me by.

On my journey back to 17 Batthany Street, I stopped several times. I stopped to breathe in the air, to absorb the sighs, the heartbeats, and the infants' cries which had frozen here under this piece of heaven a year before, and which were still lingering between heaven and earth, awaiting redemption. I could still hear the monotonous and rhythmless steps of a multitude being driven by strangers, not knowing whereto and why. Standing there, the entire road I was walking assumed the shape of a mammoth question mark. I sat down on a stone wall and, with closed eyes, stared into the vast emptiness. I hoped that someone would approach me, that someone would ask me where I was coming from, and whereto I was heading. No one came, nobody asked. Then, a big black cat came and stood beside me, gazing smilingly into my eyes. It made delicate movements with its tail as if to establish contact with me. I had never touched a cat or a dog. I had been taught that they were unclean animals and whoever touched them would become unclean and forget his studies. Now I was tempted to touch this big black cat which extended such warm friendship to me on this first day of my arrival in Szatmár. Hesitatingly, I touched the soft fur with the tip of my finger. To my surprise, the animal cuddled itself close to my foot, moving ever closer to me, all the time gazing tenderly into my eyes, emitting sounds of entreaty. I remembered the cheder stories about unfortunate souls reincarnated in unclean animals, wandering about, searching for salvation. I startled. Was this one of those trapped creatures in search of redemption? Since Minchah time had already arrived, I rubbed my hands on the grass to remove the impurities, turned to face the east, and recited Psalm 145. I prayed quietly, so as not to attract the attention of passersby. Yet when I arrived at the verse that begins with the Hebrew letter *samekh* I heard myself saying loudly; "The Lord upholdeth all who fall, and raiseth up all who are bowed down. The eyes of all look hopefully to Thee, and Thou givest them their food in due season." When I opened my eyes, I saw a handful of people standing close by, observing me in astonishment. The cat was not there. I took my rucksack and walked away, heading toward my destination.

I had no watch, nor did I pay any attention to time as I strolled, stopped, and paced again. On my way, I passed homes that I knew had belonged to Jews before the war, and I knew the people who had lived in those homes. Now I saw other people in those homes; I wondered who they were. Then I found myself approaching my old home, my last permanent abode. As I came closer, my paces increased speed, as did my heartbeats. In a few more minutes, there I was standing on the ruins of my past.

Nobody lived in the place where only a little more than a year before there had been thriving life. There was no living soul where not long ago four families had lived, nurtured hopes and fears, raised children, celebrated feasts and festivals, and wove dreams of love and life. I was met by a great emptiness and a howling silence. In all the units, there were no doors nor windows; none of the better furnishings were there. It was obvious that vandals had been at work and that they had done a thorough job. The lilac tree wasn't there, either. In its place there was a heap of rubbish.

With trepidation I entered the place that had once housed me and my family. The floors were strewn with torn books and loose pages desecrated by the elements and by the hands of vandals. Among the books I recognized some of my own, all mutilated beyond recovery.

I looked for the most valuable treasure of our family—the chest which had stored the approximately two hundred postcards written by three generations of grandparents. The chest wasn't there. How disappointed the looter must have been when, in the privacy of his home, all he found in it were some old cards written in tiny letters in a strange language.

Looking out through the gaping hole in the ceiling, I realized it was getting dark. Something in the heap of rubbish close to where I was standing moved, and I heard a rattle. I was frightened by two big glittering eyes peering at me from the darkness. It was a rat whose peace I had apparently disturbed by my unexpected intrusion. Since I was in no mood to argue with a rat, I decided to leave as quickly as I could.

Picking up my rucksack, I quietly paced toward the exit. Inadvertently, I stretched out my right hand toward the doorpost, as I had always been wont to do. Strangely, the mezuzah was still there, although somewhat damaged. The word *Shadday* on the upper part of the mezuzah, the name "Almighty," had faded away. I touched the sacred object, then, my lips, and hurried into the street.

Outside, a damp, starry night encountered me. From the direction of the Szamos River came a cool breeze and a familiar smell. A cacophony of barking dogs split the silence which was descending on the city. Never before had I heard so many dogs barking in Szatmár. I readied myself to spend my first night in my old-new hometown.

CPSIA information can be obtained at www.ICGtesting.com
Printed in the USA
BVOW072346160212

283081BV00001B/9/P